P9-DFW-984

NEW DIRECTIONS FOR TEACHING AND LEARNING

Marilla D. Svinicki, *University of Texas, Austin*
EDITOR-IN-CHIEF

Strategies for Energizing Large Classes: From Small Groups to Learning Communities

Jean MacGregor
Evergreen State College

James L. Cooper
California State University, Dominguez Hills

Karl A. Smith
University of Minnesota

Pamela Robinson
California State University, Dominguez Hills

EDITORS

Number 81, Spring 2000

JOSSEY-BASS PUBLISHERS
San Francisco

STRATEGIES FOR ENERGIZING LARGE CLASSES: FROM SMALL GROUPS TO LEARNING COMMUNITIES
Jean MacGregor, James L. Cooper, Karl A. Smith, Pamela Robinson (eds.)
New Directions for Teaching and Learning, no. 81
Marilla D. Svinicki, Editor-in-Chief

Microfilm copies of issues and articles are available in 16mm and 35mm, as well as microfiche in 105mm, through University Microfilms Inc., 300 North Zeeb Road, Ann Arbor, Michigan 48106–1346.

ISSN 0271–0633   ISBN 0–7879–5337–7

NEW DIRECTIONS FOR TEACHING AND LEARNING is part of The Jossey-Bass Higher and Adult Education Series and is published quarterly by Jossey-Bass Inc., Publishers, 350 Sansome Street, San Francisco, California 94104–1342. Periodicals postage paid at San Francisco, California, and at additional mailing offices. Postmaster: Send address changes to New Directions for Teaching and Learning, Jossey-Bass Inc., Publishers, 350 Sansome Street, San Francisco, California 94104–1342.

New Directions for Teaching and Learning is indexed in College Student Personnel Abstracts, Contents Pages in Education, and Current Index to Journals in Education (ERIC).

SUBSCRIPTIONS cost $58.00 for individuals and $104.00 for institutions, agencies, and libraries. Prices subject to change.

EDITORIAL CORRESPONDENCE should be sent to the editor-in-chief, Marilla D. Svinicki, The Center for Teaching Effectiveness, University of Texas at Austin, Main Building 2200, Austin, TX 78712–1111.

Cover photograph by Richard Blair/Color & Light © 1990.

www.josseybass.com

Printed in the United States of America on acid-free recycled paper containing 100 percent recovered waste paper, of which at least 20 percent is postconsumer waste.

CONTENTS

FROM THE SERIES EDITOR

About This Publication. Since 1980, *New Directions for Teaching and Learning (NDTL)* has brought a unique blend of theory, research, and practice to leaders in postsecondary education. *NDTL* sourcebooks strive not only for solid substance but also for timeliness, compactness, and accessibility.

The series has four goals: to inform readers about current and future directions in teaching and learning in postsecondary education, to illuminate the context that shapes these new directions, to illustrate these new directions through examples from real settings, and to propose ways in which these new directions can be incorporated into still other settings.

This publication reflects the view that teaching deserves respect as a high form of scholarship. We believe that significant scholarship is conducted not only by researchers who report results of empirical investigations but also by practitioners who share disciplined reflections about teaching. Contributors to *NDTL* approach questions of teaching and learning as seriously as they approach substantive questions in their own disciplines, and they deal not only with pedagogical issues but also with the intellectual and social context in which these issues arise. Authors deal on the one hand with theory and research and on the other with practice, and they translate from research and theory to practice and back again.

About This Volume. The current issue provides a wealth of information to inform our use of learning communities within the context of classes of all types. Since most of the new pedagogies involve the students in collaborative work, a solid understanding of how it works is key to their success.

MARILLA D. SVINICKI, editor-in-chief, is director of the Center for Teaching Effectiveness at the University of Texas, Austin.

Editors' Notes

A growing body of research points to the value of undergraduate learning environments that set high expectations, promote active and interactive learning, and give students personal validation and frequent feedback on their work. These settings and practices are especially beneficial for beginning learners as they make the transition to college. Yet at most universities, introductory courses or classes that fulfill general education requirements often carry enrollments of hundreds of students. These large-class settings have historically been heavily lecture-centered, requiring minimal student engagement and expecting little more than memorization of terms and concepts as evidence of student learning. The sheer size and anonymity of large classes seem to militate against the very elements that promote students' involvement and intellectual development, learning, and success. Inattention or absence from class, note-taking services that thrive at the edge of campus, and mediocre student performance seem to be tolerated simply as unfortunate realities.

There is little consensus on how to improve large classes. Some contend that the large-class, "tell-them-and-test-them" structure is ineffective—even corrupt—and should be jettisoned entirely in favor of smaller, more intimate classes. Others argue that as long as the reward system favors the primacy of research there will be little incentive to rethink or improve large-class teaching. Many other faculty members lay the blame on the students for their disengagement, bad manners, and lack of maturity, motivation, or skills for learning in these environments. Others still are resigned to the reality that large lower-division classes will always be needed to subsidize upper-division and graduate ones, and they think the answer lies in more charismatic lecturers, electronic technology, or both.

Meanwhile, in recent years, a growing number of college teachers have quietly been transforming their large-class settings to make them more academically and socially involving for their students. These teachers share an assumption: they believe that deeper engagement and more lasting learning arise from the active use of the concepts of the class, the construction of one's own knowledge and meaning, and the creation of a student community—right in the moment—during the class itself. Even though they are dealing with class enrollments ranging from eighty to over six hundred, these faculty members are working to develop ways to increase student involvement, active learning, higher expectations, and increased feedback.

This volume is a synthesis of interviews that we conducted with forty-eight individuals across the United States who are infusing their large classes with small-group activities or are working explicitly to create student communities within large classes. How *large* is a "large class?" For some, any class over 40 or 50 students is considered large. For others, a class of 100 students seems to be the turning point. Most of our informants are working with classes of over 100 students, and some are teaching substantially larger classes, in the 350- to 600-student range.

We need to clarify our use of terms at the outset. Some of the teachers we interviewed for this volume refer to their practices under the rubric of *collaborative learning*. Others call their strategies *cooperative learning*. Still others refer to their efforts as *group work* or *small-group activity,* or *learning teams, workshop groups,* or *learning communities.* Some faculty members are well versed in the literature on theory and practice of cooperative and collaborative learning approaches, whereas others have invented their approaches wholly on their own.

We recognize the different disciplinary roots, epistemologies, and bodies of practice of cooperative and collaborative learning, and are associated with these approaches ourselves (Jean MacGregor with collaborative learning, Jim Cooper and Karl Smith with cooperative learning). However, in this volume we have chosen not to split hairs over which approach is which, but rather to refer to these strategies generally as small-group learning. In the examples we describe, we found great variability in the structure teachers establish for their groups, in the types of intellectual tasks they pose, and in the work that students produce as a result. Yet it is in those moments that large faceless classes become small working teams and that students enter relationships with one another and with the ideas of the class. It is then that student learning and meaning-making can occur more enjoyably and more effectively. *That* is what we feel is most important, not which term is used for what is going on. Still, if readers are interested in a comparative framework for practices formally called cooperative and collaborative learning, we recommend the article, "Building Bridges Between Cooperative and Collaborative Learning," which appeared in a 1995 issue of *Change* magazine (Matthews, Cooper, Davidson, and Hawkes, 1995).

In Chapter One, Jim Cooper and Pamela Robinson describe the prevalence of large classes in universities today and review the challenges to student engagement and learning posed by large, lecture-centered settings. They go on to weave a theoretical and empirical rationale for using small-group learning. Chapters Two and Three provide descriptions of small-group learning practices in a variety of large-class environments, moving from brief, informal, "turn-to-your-neighbor" types of activities (described by Jim Cooper and Pamela Robinson) to much more complex and extended ones (described by Karl Smith). In Chapter Four, Jean MacGregor examines the emerging efforts to create stronger student communities and deeper engagement with learning through new structural approaches to extend classes with intensive supplemental workshops or to cluster multiple classes. These curriculum-restructuring efforts have the intention of fostering a sense of student belonging to a common enterprise, as well as intellectual connections between courses. Although these learning community approaches are found on campuses of all sizes, the examples described here involve only large-class environments. In Chapter Five, we draw together faculty members' responses to questions both they and we frequently are asked about both the philosophy and practice of engaging students in small-group learning in large-class settings. And finally, in Chapter Six Karl Smith and Jean MacGregor discuss the opportunities and challenges for expanding and strengthening these kinds of approaches, and suggest some major resources for faculty, both in print and on the Web.

The idea for this volume was stimulated by the late Robert Menges, former editor-in-chief of this series. He contacted us in 1997 and wondered what was next on the horizon for collaborative and cooperative learning. Our initial conversations turned almost immediately to the challenge as well as the value of building small-group learning in large-class settings and our sense that indeed this was a developing "new direction for teaching and learning." We three had enjoyed collaborating on several conferences and projects in the past decade, and we felt that working together on this volume would deepen our understanding of the special approaches and issues for faculty members working in large classes.

We are grateful to Bob Menges for his early interest in and support of this volume, and also to Marilla Svinicki for her editorial support as well as her special interest and work on strengthening large-class learning with faculty members at University of Texas-Austin.

Finally, we recognize and thank the many faculty members and administrative staff who graciously gave their time for extensive interviews about their work. They are Deborah E. Allen (University of Delaware), David Arendale (University of Missouri-Kansas City), Diana C. Archibald (University of Massachusetts-Lowell), Catherine M. Bristow (Michigan State University), Brian Coppola (University of Michigan), Monica Devanas (Rutgers University), Ann Dwyer (California State University-Los Angeles), Dewey L. Dykstra, Jr. (Boise State University), Diane Ebert-May (Michigan State University), Becky Edgerton and Phyllis S. Endicott (Northern Colorado State University), Joan Graham (University of Washington), Patricia Hauslein (St. Cloud State University), Kenneth J. Heller and Patricia M. Heller (University of Minnesota), Jean Henscheid (National Resource Center for the Freshman Year Experience and Students in Transition), Susan A. Holton (Bridgewater State College), Tony Grasha (University of Cincinnati), M. Catharine (Kay) Hudspeth (California State University-Pomona), Michael-ann Jundt (University of Washington), Calvin S. Kalman (Concordia University, Montreal), Elizabeth Keating (University of Texas at Austin), Ray Lischner (Oregon State University), Thomas R. Lord (Indiana University-Pennsylvania), John Masterson (Texas Lutheran University), Kathleen McKinney (Illinois State University), Larry Michaelson (University of Oklahoma), Craig Nelson (Indiana University), Corly Peterson (Iowa State University), Helen Place (Washington State University), Steven M. Richardson (Bowling Green State University), Johanna Seibt (University of Texas at

Austin), Mano Singham (Case Western Reserve University), Philip Sokolove (University of Maryland-Baltimore County), Marilyn Spencer, Robert Jackson, and Veronica Guzman-Hays (Texas A&M-Corpus Christi), Marilynne Stout (Pennsylvania State University-University Park), Judith Summerfield (CUNY-Queens College), Daniel Udovic (University of Oregon), Mark Urban-Lurain (Michigan State University), Robert Webking (University of Texas-El Paso), Maryellen Weimer (Pennsylvania State University-Berks Campus), Donald J. Weinshank (Michigan State University), John Wright (University of Wisconsin-Madison), Therese M. Zawacki (George Mason University), and Michael Zeileh (University of New Mexico-North).

The approaches, insights, and hard work of these individuals underpin this entire volume. Their vision and accomplishments have deepened our belief that change and reform and increased student learning are possible even under the most challenging structural conditions.

Jean MacGregor
James L. Cooper
Karl A. Smith
Pamela Robinson
Editors

Reference

Matthews, R. S., Cooper, J. L., Davidson, N., and Hawkes, P. "Building Bridges Between Cooperative and Collaborative Learning." *Change*, pp. 35–40. July–Aug. 1995.

JEAN MACGREGOR *directs a FIPSE-funded National Learning Communities Dissemination Project at The Washington Center for Improving the Quality of Undergraduate Education at The Evergreen State College. She also teaches in the master's of environmental studies program at Evergreen.*

JAMES L. COOPER *is coordinator of the teaching curriculum master's program at California State University, Dominguez Hills. He recently stepped down as editor of the* Cooperative Learning and College Teaching *newsletter, which he founded with a FIPSE grant awarded to him from 1990 to 1993.*

KARL A. SMITH *is Morse-Alumni Distinguished Teaching Professor of civil engineering at the University of Minnesota, where he teaches modeling, engineering systems, and project management. He has a split appointment with Michigan State University, where he does faculty development work.*

PAMELA ROBINSON *teaches courses in research methods and social cultural issues in the graduate education department at California State University, Dominguez Hills. She has served as associate editor of the* Cooperative Learning and College Teaching *newsletter for the past eight years.*

1

In undergraduate settings, one constellation of strategies for creating student engagement and increasing student learning involves small-group inquiry and reflection.

The Argument for Making Large Classes Seem Small

James L. Cooper, Pamela Robinson

Maria Bravo is hurrying to Dr. Robert Webking's Introduction to Politics class this warm October morning. She is among 560 students taking this fall 1998 class at the University of Texas, El Paso. She arrives a few minutes early and is given a handheld computer after presenting her student identification card to the teaching assistant.

Webking often begins the class with a short, multiple-choice quiz on the assigned reading. On this day, however, he begins by lecturing on the day's topic: the concept of freedom as articulated by Plato. After about fifteen minutes, he shows a multiple-choice question on a large overhead screen asking students whether freedom should be absolute for all human beings or whether it should be dependent on several extenuating circumstances. The class is given a minute to reflect on the question, and Maria then enters her response on the computer. Two students sitting beside her use the computer to enter their responses. Students throughout the classroom are doing the same thing, and within a minute or two Webking has hundreds of responses. These answers are tallied by the computer and shown on the screen. As Webking expects based on prior semesters' experiences, most students indicate that freedom should be absolute for all human beings. He then displays a brief cartoon of an infant crawling toward a can of Drano that is in a cupboard under a sink. The class, 65 percent of whom had chosen the absolute-freedom response, chuckle ruefully and buzz among themselves. Webking invites the students to discuss briefly, in pairs or trios, the question just posed and to determine whether they would like to change their answers. After a minute or so, he continues lecturing for another fifteen minutes before posing another question to the students.

NEW DIRECTIONS FOR TEACHING AND LEARNING, no. 81, Spring 2000 © Jossey-Bass Publishers

Webking notes that this class, composed of 70 percent Latino students (the all-campus average) has about 80 percent of the students in attendance. Before he initiated this active-learning methodology using Classtalk—the computer instructional system just described—the student attendance was about 50 percent. Webking also reports that his students' exam scores are higher since he initiated his cooperative-learning procedures and that his teaching evaluations are overwhelmingly positive. Time on task (giving full attention to the lecture or activity) has also improved, even for students sitting in the last row.

Few professors teaching large classes have the state-of-the art technology described in this vignette, which offers a slightly modified version of an actual observation of Dr. Robert Webking's class (the student name is fictitious). However, we believe that the principles of effective teaching and learning depicted here can be substantially incorporated in most large-class settings, whatever the instructional approach or physical setting.

It is safe to say that in undergraduate settings large classes are prevalent and will remain so in the foreseeable future. The pressure is on at many schools to increase class sizes further. Lecture is the prevailing teaching strategy in these classes, and in these settings students are not usually challenged to engage in much thinking or reflecting on course material. This large-class–lecture-centered approach seems to be inviting increased degrees of student disengagement. Nevertheless, we are not calling for the total abandonment of the lecture as a teaching strategy. Rather, we would like to make this approach to teaching more meaningful and engaging for students, especially in large-class settings. One constellation of strategies for creating student engagement and increasing student learning involves small-group inquiry and reflection. Can it happen in large classes? We believe so. Numbers of our colleagues are actively and successfully using these approaches. In the remainder of this chapter, we present a rationale for using small-group approaches to make large classes more engaging and productive for both students and teachers.

Large Classes and Lecture Modes: Prevailing Realities

In undergraduate settings today, large-class environments are prevalent. On many campuses, dozens of classes are regularly enrolled at over fifty students, and many carry enrollments of one hundred, two hundred, and up to six hundred and seven hundred students. The political realities of large universities are structured to have large-enrollment lower-division courses pay for small-enrollment upper-division and graduate classes. This pattern is not likely to disappear in the near future. These classes are often taught entirely in the lecture mode, with tests that often call for low levels of student understanding. Rarely are students asked to process their learning, unless the class also carries a discussion or quiz section or lab component. Even then, the discussion section is little more than a supplementary or review lecture delivered by a teaching assistant (TA). It is a sad commentary on our universities that the least engaging class sizes and the least involving pedagogy is foisted upon the students at the most pivotal time of their undergraduate careers: when they are beginning college.

The literature on students' responses to large-class learning environments is limited and not encouraging. A study conducted by Carbone and Greenberg (1998) at the University of Maryland in 1994 yielded a general dissatisfaction with the quality of large-class learning experiences. This random sampling of one hundred students revealed what bothered them the most:

• Lack of interaction with faculty members (in and out of class)
• Lack of structure in lectures
• Lack of or poor discussion sections
• Inadequate contact with teaching assistants
• Inadequacy of classroom facilities and environment
• Lack of frequent testing or graded assignments

Only 25 percent of the students agreed with the statement "The size of the class does not affect my ability to learn," whereas 41 percent strongly disagreed and another 15 percent disagreed. In another study of student perceptions of large college classes (Wulff, Nyquist, and Abbott, 1987), students noted a number of problems. They reported that there was lessened individual accountability ("It is easier to do anything you want, sleep, not attend, or lose attention"). They also commented on the impersonal nature of such classes ("No one knows I'm here"), which led to decreased motivation. A third factor associated with large classes was an increase in noise and distractions ("Rude people who come late, leave early, or sit and talk to their buddies"). Wulff, Nyquist, and Abbott conclude, "Foremost among the dimensions of large classes that hindered students' learning was the lack of instructor-student interaction with opportunities for questions and discussions." They assert, "The key seems to lie in finding ways to provide instructor-student interaction in the large-class context" (1987, p. 21).

It is no accident that these large classes are commonly referred to as "large lecture" or "large lecture sections," for faculty members generally teach the way they were taught in these settings—via the lecture. In *Redesigning Higher Education* (1994), Lion Gardiner reported on a 1980 study by Blackburn, Pellino, Boberg, and O'Connell in which 73 to 83 percent of the college teachers surveyed identified the lecture method as their usual instructional strategy. These high percentages were based on data obtained from 1800 faculty members representing a variety of institutions (large and small, public and independent, community colleges and research universities). Gardiner mentions several other studies whose conclusions are the same. Similar findings have been recently described by Horace Rockwood, the director of the Pennsylvania State University Summer Teaching Academy (personal communication with the authors, Feb. 1999). He polled 450 faculty members in the Pennsylvania State system who attended this academy and found that approximately 80 percent of them use the lecture as their primary instructional method. Rockwood's findings are compelling because these faculty members have strong commitments to teaching, as evidenced by their having enrolled in the weeklong teaching institute.

Are Lectures Effective?

Given that most of the professorate choose lecturing as their primary instructional strategy, what do we know about the efficacy of lectures? The research here is fairly consistent, and the news is not good. Pascarella and Terenzini (1991), McKeachie (1986, 1994, 1999), and others have reviewed the impact of lecturing on a variety of student outcomes. Many of these studies compare the lecture with some other form of instruction, usually a discussion method. In reviewing seventeen such comparative studies, McKeachie (1986) noted that lectures and discussion methods are equally effective in fostering memorization of lower-level factual material but that the lecture method is less effective when measures of long-term knowledge retention, transfer of knowledge to new situations, measures of higher-order thinking, attitude change, and motivation for further learning are assessed. McKeachie's findings are consistent with similar research syntheses conducted by Bligh (1972), Costin (1972), and Pascarella and Terenzini (1991).

   In their 1998 cooperative-learning workbook, Johnson, Johnson, and Smith identify additional problems with the lecture approach. They note that the lecturer makes a series of assumptions about learners that may not be justified. These assumptions are that all students are intelligent, educated persons oriented toward auditory learning; need the same information presented orally at the same time and pace, without dialogue with the presenter; have high working-memory capacities; possess the prerequisite knowledge to benefit from the lecture; and have good note-taking skills. How many colleges and universities dependent on large lecture classes make these assumptions? How many have tested them?

   One reason for the disappointing results regarding the efficacy of the lecture method may relate to the low time on task associated with lecture techniques. Penner (1984), Verner and Dickson (1967), and others have noted that time on task (paying full attention) with the lecture method is high for the first ten to twenty minutes, then tends to drop until near the end of the lecture, when according to Lloyd, attention picks up in anticipation of the end. Student note-taking thoroughness reflects similar decreases over the course of the lecture (Gardiner, 1994). The literature on retention of course content presented via lecture is even more troubling. Gardiner reports research that indicated that students retain 42 percent of lecture content when assessed immediately after the presentation; this dropped to 20 percent a week later.

Consistent with these reports of lack of student involvement and retention of information, Kuh, Schuh, and Whitt (1991) reported on a *compact of disengagement* between faculty members and students. In effect, Kuh, Schuh, and Whitt observed, faculty members in large-class environments send the message "You leave me alone and I will leave you alone" (p. 362). Large classes often set up a distance between instructors and students, where more often than not the faculty member does not know the students personally and vice versa. Students feel little sense of responsibility or accountability in class. Many attend irregularly. We often hear that large-lecture attendance dwindles throughout the term and is often down to 30 to 40 percent by the end. And in many larger classes, note-taking services have sprung up as lively businesses through which students buy lecture notes in lieu of attending class. Clearly, students across the nation are sending us signals concerning their disaffection with large classes.

Appropriate and Inappropriate Uses of the Lecture

This is not to say that the lecture is without merit. All four of the editors of this issue of *New Directions* use lectures in the classes they teach, along with other teaching strategies. Appropriate uses of the lecture, according to McKeachie (1999), Cuseo (1998), and Costin (1972) include these:

- To organize, integrate, and update reading materials
- To model problem solving and critical thinking as conducted by an advanced practitioner in the field
- To demonstrate enthusiasm for the subject matter
- To relate course-relevant personal experiences to the students
- To explain and develop complex concepts and ideas introduced in the reading
- To provide context for issues and ideas and information introduced in the reading

Johnson, Johnson, and Smith (1998) add to this list by indicating that lectures may be useful when the teacher needs to integrate information from a large variety of sources, or a number of points of view, in a small amount of time. As McKeachie (1999) noted, lecture preparation can serve as a useful tool for the teacher, requiring him or her to spend time updating, synthesizing, and reflecting on course content.

In contrast, Cuseo (1998) noted that lectures are least appropriate when material is already available and comprehensible in print; when material is of a rote nature that can be more readily processed by the learner in a text or handout; and when course content can be most effectively retained through direct, personal contact (as in public service projects or cooperative learning).

Theoretical and Empirical Rationale for Using Small Groups

This volume presents a number of small-group approaches that may be used within and as adjuncts to large-class instruction. Each approach has its own history of empirical support, ranging from relatively rich to fairly limited. We believe these strategies are reinforced by a wide range of empirical and theoretical arguments, providing a kind of convergent validity for their power. Some of these are described in this section. Additional sources documenting the power of small-group work are listed in Chapter Six.

Promoting Cognitive Elaboration. In order for students to gain mastery of academic content they need to move it into long-term memory and embed it in their own cognitive structures. For this to happen, they need to actively use the material they are learning and construct their own understanding of it, not simply read about it or hear it in a lecture. Researchers and theorists committed to constructivism, information processing, and cognitive development agree that passive involvement with course content, usually associated with the lecture method, does not provide the kind of deep learning that is needed if students are to master the content so that they can later use it flexibly and powerfully (Vygotsky, 1978; Kurfiss, 1988; Pascarella and Terenzini, 1991; Bruffee, 1993). These researchers and theorists have documented that information presented in lectures must be moved into long-term memory by having the students develop into communities of learners who discuss, debate, and summarize academic content.

Some small-group learning strategies go further than simply asking students to discuss academic concepts and ideas; they actually ask students to teach them to each other. Most people know from experience that a powerful way to learn material at a deep level is to teach it to others. Research conducted by O'Donnell and Dansereau (1992) and Ruhl, Hughes, and Schloss (1987) confirms this notion. The Roman philosopher, Seneca, said it best: *Qui docet discet:* "When you teach, you learn twice" (Whitman, 1988).

Enhancing Critical Thinking. Research and theory associated with critical thinking and developmental psychology support the concept of cognitive elaboration and development described in the previous paragraph. Developmental theorists including Piaget (1952), Vygotsky (1978), Perry (1970), Belenky, Clinchy, Goldberger, and Tarule (1986), and Gilligan (1982) stress the importance of engaging in social interactions, especially with others who are in proximal stages of cognitive development, as a means of fostering more mature ways of thinking about the world. In other words, many students learn best from other students, who can explain new information using language more understandable and less academic than a professor (this is sometimes called "converting teacher talk into student talk"). Critical-thinking researchers such as Joanne Kurfiss (1988) concur, stressing the importance of the social community of learners as a critical influence in developing higher-order thinking. Steven Brookfield, in his influential book *Developing Critical Thinkers,* noted: "When we develop critical thinkers, helping them form resource networks with others who are involved in this activity may make a crucial difference. Because identifying and challenging assumptions, and exploring alternatives, involve elements of threat and risk taking, the peer support provided by a group of others also trying to do this is a powerful psychological ballast to critical thinking efforts. Where such a network does not already exist, one of the most important tasks of those trying to facilitate critical thinking is to encourage its development" (1987, p. 79).

In his classic work *What Matters in College?* Alexander Astin (1993) provides significant support for the role of peers in fostering critical thinking. Astin assessed which elements of the college experience have the greatest impact on a host of cognitive and affective student outcomes, including measures of critical thinking. His examination of thousands of students and nearly two hundred college experiences indicates that frequency of student-student and student-faculty interactions are the best predictors of positive student outcomes.

Kurfiss (1988) indicates that developing higher-order thinking implies practice in explicitly formulating and justifying thinking, an element common to most small-group instruction described in this volume. Ahlum-Heather and DiVesta (1986) note that when students are required to explain what they do when solving a problem, they perform better on subsequent problem-solving tests. This latter finding is consistent with work by O'Donnell and Dansereau (1992), who found that in the small-group research that they performed, students *doing* the explaining achieved at a higher level on a subsequent task than students *receiving* the explanation.

Recent work in science education by Eric Mazur (1997) at Harvard and Springer, Stanne, and Donovan (1999) at the University of Wisconsin-Madison reinforce the importance of cooperative learning in fostering higher-order thinking skills. Mazur found that having students discuss their ideas with peers by using a classroom assessment technique known as ConcepTests produced significantly higher levels of physics problem solving relative to students exposed to traditional lectures (see the next chapter for more on ConcepTests). Springer and his colleagues performed a meta-analysis of the impact of small-group instruction in science, mathematics, engineering, and technology classes at the college level. In their summary of thirty-nine high-quality studies they found that academic achievement was significantly enhanced by the use of small-group instruction. Higher-order thinking was the measure of achievement used in many of the studies included in their meta-analysis.

Providing Feedback. Most of the strategies described in this volume offer students prompt and descriptive feedback on the quality of their performances. In most lecture formats, however, students have to wait weeks to practice course-related skills or to demonstrate understanding of course content and then receive feedback. For example, an instructor may present course material during week two, not assess understanding on a test or paper until week six, and then present feedback to the students in week eight or nine. Most of the strategies that we describe allow students to practice a skill or demonstrate an understanding and receive immediate feedback from other students, TAs, or faculty members, and the feedback provided is often descriptive and detailed regarding specific strengths and weaknesses.

Walberg (1984) performed a research synthesis of the kinds of educational interventions and procedures that appeared to have the most powerful impact on student outcomes. The most powerful predictor was feedback to students. In their classic report *Seven Principles for Good Practice in Undergraduate Education,* Chickering and Gamson (1987) reinforce the importance of feedback, making it one of their seven principles. Although much of Walberg's work was based on precollegiate populations, Chickering and Gamson's work was based on extensive reviews of the college-teaching literature. Indeed, these researchers and others (for example, Rosenshine and Meister, 1995) report that the model-practice-feedback loop is among the most powerful instructional strategies available to teachers at all levels. This procedure involves having the teacher model the technique, skill, or concept to be taught. Then students are given multiple opportunities to practice the skill or work with the concept soon after modeling takes place. Finally, students are given prompt and descriptive feedback on the quality of their performances.

Promoting Social and Emotional Development. The small-group structures described in this volume not only provide rich experiences that foster achievement and critical thinking but also develop affective dimensions of students, such as sense of community, altruism, self-efficacy, and learner empowerment (Johnson and Johnson, 1989; Abrami, Chambers, Poulsen, De Simone, d'Apollonia, and Howden, 1995; Belenky and others, 1986). Liking for the discipline and commitment to lifelong learning have also been linked with small-group instruction (Cuseo, 1996; Cooper and Robinson, 1999). Many national reports and blue-ribbon commissions have advised greater use of small-group work to foster these outcomes and to teach team skills—skills highly valued by employers and deeply needed in our communities (Cuseo, 1996; Johnson, Johnson, and Smith, 1998). As Katz, Bornholdt, Gaff, Hoffman, Newman, Ratner, and Weingartner (1988, p. 35) noted:

> Cooperative learning arrangements allow individual students the opportunity
> to work with others on a shared task—in pursuit of a common goal. This may
> help students to develop the types of human relations skills (for example,

active listening, empathy, consensus building, leadership, constructive conflict management and resolution) which will be relevant and transferable to similar social situations they will encounter in their future careers. The importance of modifying our traditional instructional techniques to provide today's college students with the opportunity to become more altruistic and cooperative is underscored by a recent report on higher education published by the Association of American Colleges. Recent descriptions of college students have berated their self-centeredness and even narcissism. Yet our educational institutions encourage many campus practices that make learning a private activity.

Appreciating Diversity. Possibly the most consistent student outcome associated with the use of cooperative learning is tolerance of diversity (Johnson and Johnson, 1989). Cuseo (1996) offered an explanation for this finding based on considerable work in social psychology. He reported research that suggests that intergroup contact under conditions of cooperation decrease racial prejudice and increase interracial tolerance among K–12 students (Slavin, 1980; Aronson, 1978), college students (Worchel, 1979), and workers in industrial organizations (Blake and Mouton, 1979). Cuseo (1990, 1996) also summarized research supporting the positive impact of small-group instruction on student outcome measures for a variety of student populations, including underrepresented racial and ethnic groups, adult and reentry students, commuter students, female students, and international students.

The demographic trends on our campuses indicate that our student bodies are more ethnically diverse than they have ever been, and this will not change. Yet many students report how difficult it is to communicate across the boundaries of difference and how racial tension is a troubling undercurrent on most college campuses (Levine and Cureton, 1998). Perhaps one of the most compelling rationales for small-group learning is to create classroom conditions that enable students to build bridges of communication and learn to work together.

Reducing Student Attrition. Forty percent of students who begin college do not graduate (Terenzini, 1986). This rate is significantly higher for commuter students (Pascarella and Terenzini, 1991) and underrepresented racial and ethnic groups (Ottinger, 1991). Most attrition occurs during the first year of college (Terenzini, 1986). The student attrition findings of Tinto (1993), Pascarella and Terenzini (1991), Astin (1993), and others suggest that a primary predictor of retention in college is student involvement in the communal life of the college. Regrettably, for many part-time, adult, and commuter students, relatively little time is spent in activities traditionally associated with developing community (for example, clubs, teams, fraternal and social organizations, dormitories and other group-living arrangements). For these students, the overwhelming percentage of contact with the college community occurs in the classroom. Whether commuter or residential, students can build both involvement and important social bonds through collaborative classroom work.

In addition to these key rationales for small-group work, a substantial body of research points to other outcomes associated with small-group learning, including increased self-esteem (Johnson and Johnson, 1989), enhanced psychological health (Johnson and Johnson, 1989), commitment to lifelong learning (Cooper and Robinson, 1999), improved ability to work in teams (Johnson, Johnson, and Smith, 1998), and a number of other cognitive and affective measures. We invite readers to consult the materials listed at the end of Chapter Six for additional documentation of the power of small-group instruction on an array of student outcome measures.

Bill McKeachie, "dean" of researchers in higher education, put it best when he said: "Our survey of teaching methods suggests that . . . if we want students to become more effective in meaningful learning and thinking, they need to spend more time in active, meaningful learning and thinking—not just sitting and passively receiving information" (McKeachie, Pintrich, Yi-Guang, and Smith, 1986, p. 77).

Even if college teachers are in complete agreement with McKeachie, they often associate small-group learning with small-class learning. As we travel the country presenting workshops on small-group learning, a typical response from faculty members is this: "Fine for you, but I teach a class of eighty (or one hundred, or two hundred) where these approaches just aren't possible." Many faculty members simply cannot conceive of large classes being anything but a 100 percent lecture-and-test-driven routine. But other strategies *are* possible. Many educational pioneers are working to make large classes small by systematically creating occasions for students to spend more time together in active, meaningful learning and thinking. Furthermore, these teachers are reporting to us how effective these approaches are for student engagement, student motivation, and student comprehension of course material. The next chapters in this volume describe what these pioneers are attempting to do as well as the challenges they face.

References

Abrami, P. C., Chambers, B., Poulsen, C., De Simone, C., d'Apollonia, S., and Howden, J. *Classroom Connections: Understanding and Using Cooperative Learning.* Orlando: Harcourt Brace, 1995.

Ahlum-Heather, M. E., and DiVesta, F. J. "The Effect of a Conscious Controlled Verbalization of a Transfer in Problem Solving." *Memory and Cognition,* 1986, *14*(3), 281–285.

Aronson, E. *The Jigsaw Classroom.* Thousand Oaks, Calif.: Sage, 1978.

Astin, A. *What Matters in College? Four Critical Years Revisited.* San Francisco: Jossey-Bass, 1993.

Belenky, M. F., Clinchy, B. M., Goldberger, N. R., and Tarule, J. M. *Women's Ways of Knowing: The Development of Self, Voice, and Mind.* New York: Basic Books, 1986.

Blackburn, R. T., Pellino, G. R., Boberg, A., and O'Connell, C. "Are Instructional Improvement Programs Off Target?" *Current Issues in Higher Education,* 1980, 2(1), 32–48.

Blake, R., and Mouton, J. "Intergroup Problem Solving in Organizations: From Theory to Practice." In W. Austin and S. Worchel (eds.), *The Social Psychology of Intergroup Relations*. Pacific Grove, Calif.: Brooks/Cole, 1979.

Bligh, D. A. *What's the Use of Lectures?* Hammondsworth, England: Penguin Books, 1972.

Brookfield, S. D. *Developing Critical Thinkers*. San Francisco: Jossey-Bass, 1987.

Bruffee, K. A. *Collaborative Learning*. Baltimore: Johns Hopkins University Press, 1993.

Carbone, E., and Greenberg, J. "Teaching Large Classes: Unpacking the Problem and Responding Creatively." In M. Kaplan (ed.), *To Improve the Academy*. Vol. 17. Stillwater, Okla.: New Forums Press and Professional and Organizational Development Network in Higher Education, 1998.

Chickering, A. W., and Gamson, Z. F. "Seven Principles for Good Practice in Undergraduate Education." *American Association for Higher Education Bulletin*, 1987, *39*, 3–7.

Cooper, J., and Robinson, P. "Promoting Core Skills and Lifelong Learning Through Cooperative Learning." In E. Dunne (ed.), *The Learning Society: International Perspectives on Core Skills in Higher Education*. London: Kogan Page, in press.

Costin, F. "Lecturing Versus Other Methods of Teaching: A Review of Research." *British Journal of Educational Technology*, 1972, *3*(1), 4–30.

Cuseo, J. B. *Cooperative Learning: A Pedagogy for Addressing Contemporary Challenges & Critical Issues in Higher Education*. Stillwater, Okla.: New Forums Press, 1996.

Cuseo, J. "Lectures: Their Place and Purpose." *Cooperative Learning and College Teaching*, 1998, *9*(1), 2.

Fearnley, S. "Class Size: The Erosive Effect of Recruitment on Numbers on Performance." *Quality in Higher Education*, 1995, *1*, 59–65.

Gardiner, L. F. "Redesigning Higher Education: Producing Dramatic Gains in Student Learning." ASHE-ERIC Higher Education Report No. 7. Washington, D.C.: George Washington University, 1994.

Gilligan, C. *In a Different Voice*. Cambridge: Harvard University Press, 1982.

Johnson, D. W., and Johnson, R. T. *Cooperation and Competition: Theory and Research*. Edina, Minn.: Interaction Books, 1989.

Johnson, D. W., Johnson, R. T., and Smith, K. A. *Active Learning: Cooperation in the College Classroom* (2nd ed.). Edina, Minn.: Interaction Books, 1998.

Katz, J., Bornholdt, L., Gaff, J. G., Hoffman, N., Newman, L. F., Ratner, N., and Weingartner, R. H. *A New Vitality in General Education*. Washington, D.C.: Association of American Colleges, 1988.

Kuh, G., Schuh, J. H., and Whitt, E. J. *Involving Colleges: Successful Approaches to Fostering Student Learning and Development Outside the Classroom*. San Francisco: Jossey-Bass, 1991.

Kurfiss, J. G. "Critical Thinking: Theory, Research, Practice, and Possibilities." Report no. 2. Washington, D.C.: Association for the Study of Higher Education, 1988.

Levine, A., and Cureton, J. *When Hope and Fear Collide: A Portrait of Today's College Student*. San Francisco: Jossey-Bass, 1998.

Mazur, E. *Peer Instruction: A User's Manual*. Englewood Cliffs, N.J.: Prentice Hall, 1997.

McKeachie, W. J. *Teaching Tips: A Guidebook for the Beginning College Teacher* (8th ed.). Lexington, Mass.: Heath, 1986.

McKeachie, W. J. *Teaching Tips: Strategies, Research, and Theory for College and University Teachers* (9th ed.). Lexington, Mass.: Heath, 1994.

McKeachie, W. J. *Teaching Tips: Strategies, Research, and Theory for College and University Teachers* (10th ed.). Boston: Houghton Mifflin, 1999.

McKeachie, W. J., Pintrich, P. R., Yi-Guang, L., and Smith, D.A.F. *Teaching and Learning in the College Classroom: A Review of the Research Literature*. Ann Arbor: Regents of the University of Michigan, 1986.

O'Donnell, A. M., and Dansereau, D. F. "Scripted Cooperation in Student Dyads: A Method for Analyzing and Enhancing Academic Learning and Performance." In R. Hertz-Lazarowitz and N. Miller (eds.), *Interaction in Cooperative Groups: The Theoretical Anatomy of Group Learning*. Cambridge: Cambridge University Press, 1992.

Ottinger, C. "College-Going Persistence and Completion Patterns in Higher Education: What Do We Know?" *ACE Research Briefs,* 1991, 2(3), 1–10.

Pascarella, E. T., and Terenzini, P. T. *How College Affects Students.* San Francisco: Jossey-Bass, 1991.

Penner, J. *Why Many College Teachers Cannot Lecture.* Springfield, Ill.: Thomas, 1984.

Perry, W. G. *Forms of Intellectual and Ethical Development During the College Years.* Austin, Tex.: Holt, Rinehart and Winston, 1970.

Piaget, J. *The Origins of Intelligence in Children.* (M. Cook, trans.). New York: Norton, 1952.

Rosenshine, B. V., and Meister, C. "Scaffolds for Teaching Higher-order Cognitive Strategies." In A. C. Ornstein (ed.), *Teaching: Theory into Practice.* Needham Heights, Mass.: Allyn & Bacon, 1995.

Ruhl, K., Hughes, C., and Schloss, R. "Using the Pause Procedure to Enhance Lecture Recall." *Teacher Education and Special Education,* 1987, 10(1), 14–18.

Slavin, R. E., "Cooperative Learning." *Review of Educational Research,* 1980, 50, 315–342.

Springer, L., Stanne, M., E., and Donovan, S. "Effects of Small-Group Learning on Undergraduates in Science, Mathematics, Engineering, and Technology: A Meta-Analysis." *Review of Educational Research,* 1999, 69(1), 50–80.

Terenzini, P. T. "Retention Research: Academic and Social Fit." Paper presented at the meeting of the southern regional office of the College of Entrance Examination Board, New Orleans, 1986.

Tinto, V. *Leaving College: Rethinking the Causes and Cures for Student Attrition* (2nd ed.). Chicago: University of Chicago Press, 1993.

Verner, C., and Dickson, G. "The Lecture: An Analysis and Review of Research." *Adult Education,* 1967, 17, 85–100.

Vygotsky, L. S. *Mind and Society.* Cambridge: Harvard University Press, 1978.

Walberg, H. "Improving the Productivity of America's Schools." *Educational Leadership,* 1984, 41(8), 19–27.

Whitman, N. A. "Peer Teaching: To Teach Is to Learn Twice." Report no. 4. Washington, D.C.: Association for the Study of Higher Education, 1988.

Worchel, S. "Cooperation and the Reduction of Intergroup Conflict: Some Determining Factors." In W. Austin and S. Worchel (eds.), *The Social Psychology of Intergroup Relations.* Pacific Grove, Calif.: Brooks/Cole, 1979.

Wulff, D. H., Nyquist, J. D., and Abbott, R. D. "Students' Perceptions of Large Classes." In M. Weimer (ed.), *Teaching Large Classes Well.* New Directions for Teaching and Learning, no. 32. San Francisco: Jossey-Bass, 1987.

2

*Through brief in-class discussions that begin, end, or
punctuate a lecture, students can prepare for the lecture,
check their understanding, or refocus on the material
presented. Faculty or teaching assistants can check for
understanding as well.*

Getting Started: Informal Small-Group Strategies in Large Classes

James L. Cooper, Pamela Robinson

I got started with discussion pairs in chemistry about ten years ago when I took over teaching the big introductory classes of several hundred students. I got started gradually by working a problem with the students and then giving the students one to work on themselves together with their neighbors sitting next to them. Now these activities underpin every class I teach. What propelled me into this was watching colleagues in lecture working a problem on the board: I saw it going into the students' eyes, down their arms and into their notebooks, but their *understanding* of the problem was bypassing their brains! Over and over, I saw the students not be able to do similar problems in the tutorial the very next day [Helen Place, personal interview with the authors, Sept. 1998].

Helen Place and dozens of other teachers of large classes are finding great success in using informal, small-group strategies in class—that is, short in-class discussions of the turn-to-your-neighbor variety that begin or end the lecture or punctuate it at key points along the way. Students are given a question or problem to consider or work through, discuss with a neighbor, and sometimes report back to the class as whole. Through these short activities, which usually take only a few minutes of class time, students can check their understanding, prepare for the lecture to come, or refocus on material just presented. As they listen in on these conversations, teachers and teaching assistants can check student understanding as well.

Interest in the use of informal, small-group strategies has grown at a rate that outstrips even the very significant growth in more formal small-group procedures (Kagan, 1994). Such work with pairs or teams is easy to implement because faculty members do not need to spend significant time devising ways to create groups or developing and coaching effective group dynamics over time. Usually there is no expectation of work to be turned in, so the teacher is not concerned with grading collaborative student work. Teachers with strong concerns about content coverage often prefer these short, informal strategies because they consume, at most, just a few minutes of their lectures.

We believe that turning over a relatively small percentage of the total in-class instructional time to informal small-group work can produce a large "bang for the buck" in making conventional lecture-centered formats more engaging for students and more productive for their learning. With these brief activities, there is little risk that teachers will lose control of their classes or encounter other forms of student resistance, an objection faculty sometimes raise against more formal small-group procedures. Once instructors have experienced success with informal strategies, they are often more inclined to commit to more elaborate small-group approaches.

A large number of informal cooperative and collaborative approaches have been identified (Kagan, 1994). In this chapter we describe a few of the most popular. We also identify critical points when these strategies might be used in class. A powerful argument for informal strategies is that they can be used in virtually any course or discipline, in introductory as well as advanced classes, and at many stages of the instructional sequence.

Examples of Informal Small-Group Strategies

Probably the most popular and influential of informal small-group approaches is think-pair-share (Lyman, 1981). In this strategy the teacher lectures for a period of time, then poses a question, test item, or issue for students to consider in brief individually (the think phase). Then, individuals turn to others sitting nearby and share their responses with another person (the pair phase). If time permits, several of the pairs share their responses with the class (the share phase).

In the think phase of think-pair-share, it is entirely possible that 100 percent of the learners are simultaneously engaged in active thinking. In the pair phase, there is the potential that at any given moment, 50 percent of the students are actively engaged in talking and problem solving. Compare this with the lecture technique, where it is often only the teacher who is engaged in active academic effort. An additional benefit of think-pair-share is that it is a natural classroom assessment technique, or CAT (Angelo and Cross, 1993). Using think-pair-share not only engages learners in what can be higher-order thinking but also provides an immediate gauge of the degree and quality of student understanding of course content. Teachers can then shape the remaining lecture time based on this feedback. At the same time, students are getting immediate and explicit feedback on the strength or weakness of their understanding. Prompt and descriptive feedback has been identified as one of the best predictors of powerful teaching and learning (Walberg, 1984; Chickering and Gamson, 1987).

A variation of think-pair-share is think-pair-square, where pairs of students share their information within teams of four rather than with the class. This strategy can be a more efficient use of class time in that the last phase of the technique tends to engage more students in active learning and conversation than the share phase of think-pair-share, where only one student at a time is reporting out to the class.

Many other informal small-group techniques are variations of think-pair-share. For example, Eric Mazur (1997), professor of physics at Harvard, has developed ConcepTests, which he integrates into his peer instruction teaching approach. About every fifteen to twenty minutes, Mazur poses a multiple-choice (ConcepTest) question that requires conceptual understanding (such as estimating the displacement of a toy boat in a bathtub). Students write their answers on a sheet and identify their levels of confidence in the answer. Then they work in pairs, attempting to convince others of their answers. Students then answer the question a second time and report their confidence levels again. Mazur then polls the whole class about their answers and uses this information in structuring the remainder of the lecture. Mazur has collected data on the impact of his approach on several outcome measures. He found that students who had ConcepTests within the lecture performed better on course exams and also scored higher on measures of traditional problem solving and conceptual understanding than students in traditional lecture classes. (See Chapter Six for Mazur's physics Web site address and that of a related University of Wisconsin chemistry Web site.)

Robert Webking's approach to teaching political science at the University of Texas, El Paso, described in Chapter One, was adapted from Mazur's ConcepTest. Michael Zeilek at the University of Northern New Mexico uses the technique in his astronomy class of several hundred. The polling of the class can be done after individual work or after pairs have compared answers. We believe that all students should be encouraged to commit publicly to an answer because letting students "off the hook" defeats the purpose of the class poll.

Susan Prescott Johnston and Jim Cooper (Johnston and Cooper, 1997) have extended Lyman's think-pair-share approach by identifying the cognitive outcomes to be developed within a class, then structuring their small-group strategies, called Quick-thinks, to assess these outcomes in order to teach them clearly and directly. Thus, it is both a teaching technique and a classroom assessment strategy. Here are some examples of Quick-thinks:

- *Reorder the steps:* Students must correctly order a set of randomly sequenced steps.
- *Paraphrase the idea:* Students are asked to explain something in their own words, often to a specific audience, such as another student, a parent, or

a client. This calls for cognitive elaboration skills as students explain the idea to others, a skill strongly related to deep learning.

- *Correct the error:* Students find the error in an inaccurate statement, a weak argument, or an illogical conclusion.
- *Support a statement:* Students must support a statement made by the teacher, using a variety of sources, which might include lecture notes, homework assignments, life experience or library research.
- *Select the response:* This a multiple-choice format similar to Mazur's ConcepTest.

Johnston and Cooper have presented these strategies to several hundred faculty members in the last two years and report that faculty in virtually all disciplines find one or more of them to be of immediate use. The approaches do not require elaborate planning, careful introduction, or coaching of students, which might be needed in more formal procedures, but they should be carefully planned and implemented, like any teaching strategy.

Another informal assessment strategy is the minute paper. As described by Robert Wilson at Berkeley (Wilson, 1986), the minute paper involves having students answer two questions in the last one to three minutes of class. One frequent question is, "What was the most important thing you learned during this class?" Another frequent question is, "What issue or concept remains muddy, or raises questions for you?" Minute papers can be used at the beginning of class in reference to homework assignments, in assessing what reading material was clear and what was not, or as a prompt for a think-pair-share activity at the end of class to identify what was clear and what was unclear about the lecture.

Psychologist Donald Dansereau at the Texas Christian University uses a highly structured approach to small-group instruction, which he calls scripted cooperative learning. After fifteen to twenty minutes of lecture, students are paired by the teacher so that teammates vary from one class session to the next. Students review class notes, taking turns as recaller-summarizer and checker. The recaller summarizes the content of the prior lecture segment and the checker assesses the summarizer's accuracy and detail. After determining the accuracy of the notes, students jointly work on developing strategies that will help them remember the content, such as constructing examples and developing mnemonic or memory devices to assist in long-term retention.

Dansereau has also examined the use of concept maps to aid in understanding and retaining content. Concept or knowledge maps are two-dimensional networks that interrelate important concepts (O'Donnell, 1994). They draw the student's attention to the overall structure of the lecture, often reducing the complexity of learning the lecture material by creating visual images of key topics and ideas and key relationships among them.

Using rigorously designed, short-term studies, Dansereau, Angela O'Donnell, and their colleagues (O'Donnell and Dansereau, 1992) have amassed a significant amount of data that indicate that their procedures result in better performance on a variety of cognitive and affective outcome measures (many relating to technical and scientific information) and transferred to individually completed tasks. They assert that teacher-structured small-group work produces better outcomes than student-structured pair activities. There is considerable difference of opinion (and sometimes outright debate) about how structured small-group work should be, and who (teachers or students) should be responsible for deciding how the given problem or intellectual task should be attacked. Our view is that these design choices depend on a variety of factors, including the course, level, discipline, teacher, specific learning outcomes, students' prior experience with small-group learning, and the point in the sequence of instruction.

Applications of Small-Group Approaches

Small-group approaches can be used successfully in many different ways.

Launching Class in Discussion. Small-group work can be used at the beginning of class to provide students with a motivation hook or an anticipatory set for what is to follow. In Jim Cooper's lecture on sampling, he often begins by asking students to "identify the error" in describing the *Literary Digest's* presidential poll of 1936, which drew from a population that had telephones and car license plates (a sample of relatively affluent people during that Depression year). When Franklin Roosevelt won the election, and not Alf Landon (as the *Digest* had predicted), the practice of biased sampling of voters became a public scandal. Making this a simple Quick-think or think-pair share activity serves to stimulate interest in a lecture on sampling theory—a boring topic for most students. To increase the likelihood that students do the reading, Robert Webking often gives ConcepTests on homework assignments at the beginning of his political science classes. He reports that his students begin to anticipate and prepare for ConcepTests and are thus better able to gain from the lecture and group work that are subsequently presented. As noted earlier, Helen Place launches her chemistry classes at Washington State University by displaying a problem on the overhead; students work through the problem and share answers with neighbors in the four-hundred-seat lecture hall, knowing that the lecture for the day will build on some concept underlying the problem. Faculty members who regularly start class with these kinds of activities report that the class feels more focused and attentive, with everyone thinking and talking about important course content right at the outset.

Breaking Up the Lecture for Comprehension Checks. As Craig Nelson (personal interview with the authors, June 1998), an Indiana University biologist puts it, these informal strategies "always work!" Although this sounds a bit overconfident, Jim Cooper generally shares this view, with some obvious caveats. It has been Cooper's experience that after fifteen to thirty minutes of lecture—particularly in his graduate research methods class—the energy level and sense of involvement that follows from the most informal of small-group tasks always increases. When attention spans are waning and yawns are waxing, he often inserts a brief think-pair-share, even if it is only something as simple as "Think of two real-world examples of random sampling," or "Now that I have drawn two correlation scatter plots, you construct a third using the data that I am writing on the board."

Tony Grasha (psychology, University of Cincinnati), Brian Coppola (chemistry, University of Michigan), Craig Nelson (biology, University of Indiana), and Helen Place (chemistry, Washington State University) are among those who regularly use informal strategies midway through the lecture. These often serve as comprehension checks for students and as classroom assessments for faculty, allowing teachers to modify the next part of their lectures appropriately.

Closing Class with Small-Group Conversation. Too often, the last few minutes of class is spent in paper-shuffling and backpack-filling, behaviors not associated with high levels of student engagement. If students come to expect a brief classroom assessment during the last few minutes of class, this off-task behavior is reduced or pushed to the very last moments of class sessions. Minute papers are particularly helpful here. Then, if they are briefly scanned by the instructor before the next class meeting, students feel that they have a voice in the class and there is a sense of continuity from one class meeting to the next. Many faculty members reduce the number of minute papers they have to check by asking students to create them in pairs or teams.

Reviewing for Exams. We have found exam review to be one of the best uses of both formal and informal small-group work, particularly for instructors new to collaborative learning. Students are usually highly motivated because they will be tested on this material very soon. In fact, we have found that students often ask for additional problem sets to take home and often stay after class for long periods of time when they feel that understanding sample questions may result in increased test performance. Another variety of this reviewing-for-the-test strategy is to have students construct their own sample test problems. Then, in pairs and teams, students attempt to answer the questions or critique them for quality.

Debriefing Exams. Giving feedback to students on exams is one of the least pleasant parts of teaching. Debriefing exams in pairs or teams makes the process a learning experience. Often, better students can explain why an answer was inaccurate or incomplete in a way that is understandable and easier to accept than if comparable information is offered by professors. Pamela Robinson gives exams back in team folders. Students then spend a few minutes explaining their answers to teammates in groups of four. Students may only question their grades on the tests after they have engaged in these discussions. Robinson reports that she gets very few complaints and that the few minutes during which small groups go over the exams is spent in high-level discussions about why answers are correct or incorrect.

Deepening Audiovisual Presentations. It is our experience that video, slide, and other AV presentations are too often used by students as opportunities to sleep or engage in other off-task activity. We have found that by involving students in brief informal work at the beginning and end of the presentations, they become more attentive and engaged. For example, in a sociology class students might be asked to predict the leading causes of prejudice or the most important influences on adolescent development, then check their responses after the film or video is shown. Or students might be given a set of questions to frame the video, then engage in team and whole-class discussion after it.

Predicting Processes and Outcomes of Demonstrations. Lorena Tribe, professor of chemistry at the University of Wisconsin-Madison, uses ConcepTests in her chemistry class of several hundred. She asks students to make predictions concerning the results of experiments, which often are vivid depictions of a chemical process. Following the experiment she has students assess their predictions. In a tape about ConcepTests produced by the university, students in her chemistry class are asked to predict if coffee will lose its color, taste, and smell when subjected to a distillation process. After pairs make their predictions, Tribe conducts the demonstration and has a pair of students taste the coffee to assess the accuracy of the predictions. This activity illustrates how an interesting demonstration can have even greater impact when combined with an informal small-group exercise.

A Period of Adjustment

Every teacher we spoke with commented that even for these short in-class tasks, there was a learning curve for the students, an adjustment time at the beginning of the term. Students are accustomed to sitting through lectures without extending themselves much to work problems or engage in complex-thinking tasks. So asking them to think hard about something, to work a problem, to make a choice, to discuss with a neighbor—all of this pushes students into a different way of being in a class. Many of them have been taught that all their learning must be individual; working with partners in a class is tantamount to cheating. As Helen Place comments,

> You have to train your students to do this; they don't come by it naturally. You have to be patient. Students do not collaborate naturally. They have been taught to compete, and not work together. . . . When I explain what I am doing with the class, I make an analogy to any sport. I tell the class that I can solve these chemistry problems and they can't—yet. The only way they can learn to do it is to do it for themselves. I say to them, "I am making you practice, just like practicing for football." This is directed, coaching practice,

which, after a while, leads to competence. . . . It usually takes me about half the semester before students really get into the rhythm of working problems with their neighbors in class. Those that go on to the second-semester chemistry classes are all ready to go, of course [personal interview with the authors, Sept. 1998].

References

Angelo, T. A., and Cross, K. P. *Classroom Assessment Techniques: A Handbook for College Teachers* (2nd ed.). San Francisco: Jossey-Bass, 1993.

Chickering, A. W., and Gamson, A. F. *Seven Principles for Good Practice in Undergraduate Education.* Racine, Wis.: Johnson Foundation/Wingspread, 1987.

Johnston, S., and Cooper, J. "Quick-thinks: Active-thinking Tasks in Lecture Classes and Televised Instruction." *Cooperative Learning and College Teaching,* 1997, 8(1), 2–7.

Kagan, S. *Cooperative Learning.* San Juan Capistrano, Calif.: Resources for Teachers, 1994.

Lyman, F. "The Responsive Class Discussion." In A. S. Anderson (ed.), *Mainstreaming Digest.* College Park: College of Education, University of Maryland, 1981.

Mazur, E. *Peer Instruction: A User's Manual.* Englewood Cliffs, N.J.: Prentice Hall, 1997.

O'Donnell, A. M. "Facilitating Scripted Cooperation Through the Use of Knowledge Maps." *Cooperative Learning and College Teaching,* 1994, 4(2), 7–10.

O'Donnell, A. M., and Dansereau, D. F. "Scripted Cooperation in Student Dyads: A Method for Analyzing and Enhancing Academic Learning and Performance." In R. Hertz-Lazarowitz and N. Miller (eds.), *The Theoretical Anatomy of Group Learning.* Cambridge: Cambridge University Press, 1992.

Walberg, H. "Improving the Productivity of America's Schools." *Educational Leadership,* 1984, 41(8), 19–27.

Wilson, R. C. "Improving Faculty Teaching: Effective Use of Student Evaluations and Consultants." *Journal of Higher Education,* 1986, 57(2), 192–211.

3

Extended small-group learning strategies such as jigsaw, structured controversy, and problem-based learning have proven so effective to many faculty members that they have moved to redesign their large classes to center around small-group learning.

Going Deeper: Formal Small-Group Learning in Large Classes

Karl A. Smith

To teach is to engage students in learning; thus teaching consists of getting students involved in the active construction of knowledge. A teacher requires not only knowledge of subject matter but knowledge of how students learn and how to transform them into active learners. Good teaching, then, requires a commitment to systematic understanding of learning. . . . The aim of teaching is not only to transmit information but also to transform students from passive recipients of other people's knowledge into active constructors of their own and others' knowledge. The teacher cannot transform without the student's active participation, of course. Teaching is fundamentally about creating the pedagogical, social, and ethical conditions under which students agree to take charge of their own learning, individually and collectively [Christensen, Garvin, and Sweet, 1991, pp. xiii, xv, xvi].

This quote from the introduction to *Education for Judgment,* one of the most highly regarded books on case-method learning, advocates compellingly for the notion that meaningful learning develops from the active construction of knowledge. Many faculty members, impressed by the impact of short-term informal group activities in their classes, are moving to adopt more formal small-group learning arrangements and to ask those student groups to undertake more complex intellectual problems and tasks. This chapter describes some of these activities, proceeding from some that are slightly more involved than those described in Chapter Two to complex in-class activities and strategies that involve massive reorganization of large classes. The types of implementation that we will describe are as follows:

- Informal strategies with extensions
- In-class project work
- Jigsaw strategies
- Structured academic controversy
- Base groups
- Problem-based learning
- Restructured lecture-recitation-laboratory
- Eliminated lecture, substitution of hands-on laboratory

Informal Strategies with Extensions

Many faculty desire more extensive student involvement after successfully implementing informal, short-term, ad hoc grouping strategies. In this chapter we describe extensions of these strategies that incorporate more detailed individual preparation before student discussion in pairs or threes, several back-and-forth conversations between small groups and the whole class, and specific role assignments to the group structure, as well as many other extensions.

Most of the faculty interviewed for this chapter have expanded on the informal cooperative learning strategy commonly known as "turn to your neighbor," which is described in Chapter Two. Calvin Kalman, professor of physics at Concordia University, Montreal, deepens this procedure in his calculus-based physics course with one hundred students by involving them in extensive individual journal-writing assignments (Calvin Kalman, personal interview with the author, Oct. 1998; Kalman and Kalman, 1996). Students write about material before the class, produce a critique based on the concepts they have come to understand after the week's classes, and develop an overview of the course with the assistance of two student reviewers at the end of the semester. Students are assigned to collaborative groups of three or four and are given a specific role—reporter, scribe, timekeeper, or critic—that is rotated. They write individually and then work together to arrive at a decision with a rationale in their groups. Kalman samples the groups' decisions, compares and contrasts what they come up with, and works to create consensus and understanding with the whole class.

Several faculty members mentioned using the bookends procedure to provide a structure for these turn-to-your-neighbor student conversations (see Figure 3.1). The bookends procedure usually begins with an engagement activity—a question or task that both sparks the students' curiosity and helps the instructor discover what they already know about the material. A simple and commonly used engagement activity is, "List at least three insights you gained from the reading assignment and at least one question." The middle part is a series of back-and-forth transitions between the instructor talking and students working individually and then in pairs or threes. The final bookend activity is a guided reflection on the class using

Figure 3.1. Informal Cooperative Learning and the Lecture

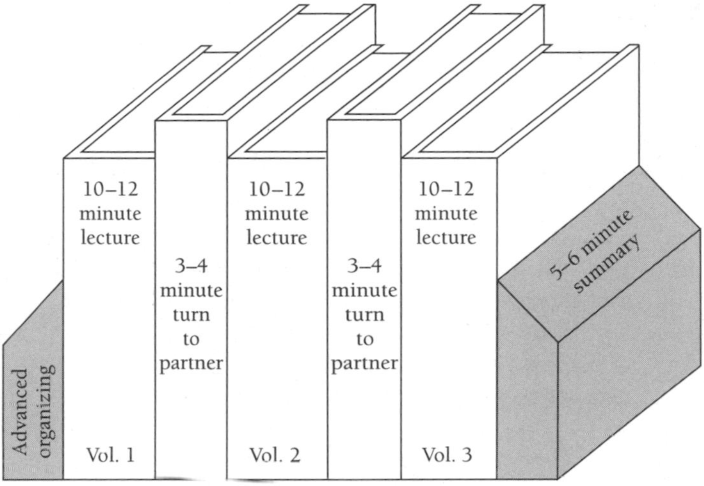

questions such as, "What were the most important concepts today?" or "What was the muddiest point?" or "Explain the following concept in your own words." These and several additional questions may be found in Angelo and Cross (1993).

A few instructors combined the bookends procedure with permanent, fixed membership groups in order to create more cohesiveness and to deepen the level of conversation. Mano Singham, professor of physics at Case Western Reserve University, divides the 220 students in his Physics 121 into permanent groups after the first class. He forms the groups so students can conveniently meet outside of class, and he sends students an e-mail message with the group information before the second class so they can sit with the other members of their group. Three to four times per class, he poses questions or problems that stress some subtlety or difficulty worthy of a group discussion. A randomly selected individual in a randomly selected group is asked to present that group's answer. Others in the group may pitch in at this stage to help with the explanation. Once a week Singham assigns an outside-of-class group homework assignment that is submitted and evaluated.

Here are the specifics about group work rules that Singham gives his students (Mano Singham, personal interview with the author, Jan. 1999):

- Group members should sit together in lectures and recitations. When a question is asked in lecture, they should pool their ideas so that the one who is called on can use the knowledge of the entire group.

- Group members should exchange names and e-mail address (or addresses and phone numbers) with one another so that they can contact one another easily.
- Each individual's name and group number should be written on all assignments and exams that are handed in.
- Individual homework assignments should be handed in separately, but they can and should be discussed with others before being handed in.
- For group homework, only one assignment per group should be handed in.
- All assignments will be returned clipped together by group. The first member of the group to come to class should pick up the assignments for that group and distribute them to the other members.
- If a member of the group is absent, another member should collect his or her assignment and any handouts and give them to the absent student as soon as possible, along with lecture notes for that day.
- Only one member should pick up any handout for the whole group.

Singham highlights the importance of cooperation in his class by asking that each group have a private meeting with him at the beginning of the semester. In this way, he can get to know the students and give them an opportunity to voice any concerns. His use of an absolute grading system underscores the cooperative learning as he states emphatically in the syllabus: "Your grade for this course will *not* depend on how well your performance compares with that of the other students. You are *not* in competition with your peers. Conversely, you will find that you will do better if your fellow students do well too" (Mano Singham, personal interview with the author, Jan. 1999).

Diane Ebert-May, professor of botany and director of the Lyman Briggs School (a residential science college) at Michigan State University, uses a learning cycle model to involve her students during large introductory biology classes. The learning cycle model of instruction she uses is based on five phases: the *engagement phase* begins with a question to probe students' prior knowledge and help organize their thinking for subsequent activities; the *exploration phase* provides students with a common basis for understanding the concepts, processes, and skills for the topic being considered; the *explanation phase* builds on the engagement and exploration phases so that students can demonstrate their understanding of concepts with additional examples; the *elaboration phase* challenges students' conceptual understanding and skills; and in the *evaluation phase* students are given an individual or group quiz (short-answer format) daily to evaluate their understanding (Ebert-May, Brewer, and Allred, 1997).

Ebert-May and colleagues have conducted systematic experimentation on this cooperative learning cycle approach. They found that students in the experimental sections had significantly higher scores on process questions (conceptual understanding of a testable scientific question, designing a method for answering the question, interpreting quantitative relationships, and explaining results) and confidence, and similar scores on content questions compared with students in a traditional lecture section (Ebert-May, Brewer, and Allred, 1997).

In-Class Project Work

The faculty members whose stories are included in this section used assigned, relatively permanent groups of students who worked together both inside and outside of class. Compared with the periodic short-term group exercises described in the previous section, these exercises are longer-term, more hands-on, and more complex.

Steve Richardson (personal interview with the author, Oct. 1998), formerly professor of geology at Iowa State University, stresses the importance of hands-on activities in the nonmajor geology classes. He randomly assigned the 240 to 250 students to permanent groups of about 6 and provided them with a group folder in which he placed the syllabus and other handouts. During a typical class period he provided each group with a box of minerals and a set of photos or showed a video clip or set of slides. He asked the groups to "handle" the materials and perform a set of prescribed tasks or respond to a set of questions. He reports that the five- to fifteen-minute exercises made a great difference in his classes. He used twelve-minute individual quizzes and then provided five minutes for a group answer, and like many of the faculty members we interviewed, underscored the importance of an absolute grading scale. As a result of these activities, attendance rose to over 90 percent and the dropout rate declined to less than 2 percent.

In his classes of 144 students in Conceptual Physics, Dewey Dykstra of Boise State University (personal interview with the author, Oct. 1998) stimulates intense group discussion by inducing a sense of "disequilibration." Catherine Fosnot, professor of education at City College of the City University of New York (1989) describes a classroom implementation of cognitive disequilibrium as follows: "I [the teacher] point out exceptions that I'm aware of that cause problems for your [the student] rules, and I try to foster debates and discussion. By arguing and testing out ideas in groups, we come up with exceptions for each other to consider, and that also promotes construction" (p. 53).

In Dykstra's classes, disequilibration is usually introduced during the two-hour lab session, where students work in groups of four. It is then dealt with during one or both of the seventy-five-minute discussion periods that are held each week. Dykstra's students develop what for them is a new ray model of light and compare the models with the actual behavior of light, images, and lenses. In so doing the students experience disequilibration because they learn that the actual behavior of light challenges their present understanding of and beliefs about light, images, and lenses. Dykstra uses in-class group discussion to help students struggle with this disequilibration but tries to stay out of the resulting discussions by maintaining the role of moderator or referee. He interacts with groups but resists telling them what they should think, although he does make specific suggestions and requests concerning process (Dykstra, Boyle, Franklin, and Monarch, 1992; Dykstra, 1996). He began using this approach because he "wanted to have an impact, especially on the preservice teachers who take the course . . . to induce as many instances of conceptual change as possible, about the content, about science, about the nature of knowledge, and about their own personal meaning" (Dewey Dykstra, personal interview with the author, Oct. 1998).

Elizabeth Keating, professor of anthropology at the University of Texas at Austin, uses a combination of in-class project groups with out-of-class project assignments in two classes, Language in Culture and Society, and Culture and Communication, whose enrollments are routinely from sixty to one hundred students. She wants students to become involved in doing research on language both to make them more active learners and to teach analytical skills. In a typical assignment she asks students, in teams, to videotape people talking in technologically rich environments to see if or how language practices are influenced by technology and whether technology influences language practices. Their observations form the basis of an analytical paper that they turn in at the end of class. The students choose their own research sites around campus and are encouraged to use the concepts discussed in class in their projects. In class, Keating breaks students into small groups of three to discuss readings and to do language analysis using overhead slides made from their own transcripts of videotaped interaction (Elizabeth Keating, personal interview with the author, Jan. 1999).

Johanna Seibt, professor of philosophy at the University of Texas at Austin, uses a research group format in her Introduction to Philosophy class, which enrolls between 150 and 350 students. The present implementation of the instructional format, as well as the didactic-epistemological perspective it is based on, was developed in collaboration with Phil Hopkins (professor of philosophy as Southwestern University). Seibt began to employ various research group formats when she noticed that "students had the most satisfying and productive learning experience during office hours when I, to shorten the line, invited them in in small groups and started a discussion about the subject instead of simply answering their questions one by one." Now, from the perspective of great success with this approach, she comments,

> My goals may sound very ambitious but they are, I believe, the only possible ones for introductory philosophy courses. I am trying to initiate or boost a movement toward intellectual maturation, radically discouraging the "cramming and regurgitating" attitude. Instead I want my students to interact critically with their readings, to engage with the problems they encounter in their reading at a cognitive and even existential level. Even though I spend much

time on teaching the tools of critical analysis and want my students to experience their intellectual independence with respect to dogmatically presented worldviews, I also want them to move beyond the easy route of skeptical relativism . . . and to understand that there is a third alternative between dogmatism and relativism, between getting "the" answer to life's important questions and getting no answer. I want them to experience that we receive concrete answers that are even the right answers for a particular context of questioning insofar—but only insofar—as we manage to sustain the activity of asking these questions [Johanna Seibt, personal interview with the author, Jan. 1999].

Seibt describes her expectations and the course structure in a detailed handout titled "How to Study in This Course." Borrowing several metaphors from the Star Trek television series, the document opens with the following challenge:

Philosophy is a subject matter that is difficult to pick up. This is not because there is so much to memorize or because one has to go through difficult calculations—in fact, as you will see, you will have to learn just a handful of new concepts, and the thinking to be done is quite simple. Rather, philosophy is a hard subject because understanding and doing philosophy requires that you adopt a new way of thinking. This new way of thinking—or better, a new cognitive attitude, a new mental posture—is best acquired by working in small groups. . . . Philosophy is often described as the adventure of thinking, but it is perhaps even better described as the adventure of *thinking together*. . . . Picture our course as a kind of flight of ideas, a mission to seek out new worlds and explore new conceptualizations, to boldly think what almost no one has thought before. Class (the lecture) is like the mother ship that carries you into various regions of the deep space of philosophical thought. The real adventure begins, however, when you get on an away team, and explore the contents of that region under your own command, making contact with what may appear alien to you in and about philosophy.

Seibt assigns students to permanent groups of four and she refers to the groups as "away teams" or journal groups. The groups meet during class and also schedule a weekly two-hour meeting outside of class. Each member of each team performs one of four roles—text researcher, life researcher, editor, and critic—that are rotated. The text researcher looks up definitions, compares definitions, searches for articles or Web sites, writes up the results, and e-mails them to the other group members. The life researcher interviews people, summarizes the results, and e-mails them to the rest of the group. The editor takes notes during group meetings and writes up the week's entries in the group's journal. The critic becomes active after receiving the data from the text researcher and the life researcher, summarizing the group's responses in the journal. Each week the groups submit their journals to the TA via e-mail and receive e-mail comments from the TA in response.

Seibt emphasizes that her redesigned courses are more consistent with professional philosophy, which has been done in groups since antiquity, and she reports extraordinary individual successes: "The particular format of the away teams, with specific rotating roles assigned to each member, should take care of differences in self-affirmation. I had one student in an upper-division course who was *extremely* shy, to the extent that I wondered about her professional future. She was just accepted to law school in Georgetown and wrote me that the research group format in my classes had turned things around for her" (Johanna Seibt, personal interview with the author, Jan. 1999).

Jigsaw Strategies

Jigsaw strategies have been used by highly effective student study groups for some time in content-dense disciplines such as medicine and law. They have been used on an ad hoc basis for many years to help all students learn an enormous amount of new conceptual material. First described by Elliot Aronson in 1978, the jigsaw procedure involves students working in a cooperative group where each student is responsible for learning a portion of the material and conscientiously teaching it to the rest of the group. The professor's role in a jigsaw involves carefully choosing the material to be "jigsawed," structuring the groups, providing a clear cooperative context for their working together, monitoring to ensure high-quality learning and group functioning, and helping students summarize, synthesize, and integrate the conceptual material. A typical template for a cooperative jigsaw is shown in Exhibit 3.1. An example of detailed guidance for learning in a jigsaw format is available in Smith (1996).

Many faculty report that the jigsaw approach provides a pleasant alternative to the lecture in helping students learn conceptual material and that it fosters interdependence among them. Although it takes preparation and time to set up the jigsaw, students usually learn more material and remember it longer, and become experienced in a procedure that they often begin using on their own.

Cathy Bristow, professor of entomology at Michigan State University, makes extensive use of the jigsaw strategy in her large life science classes (Bristow, 1995). She does a five-week case study on Mad Cow disease, currently a hot issue with many interdisciplinary elements. She asks her students to work in "research teams" to investigate and then prepare a report on Mad Cow disease, incorporating perspectives on the history, molecular biology, epidemiology, agricultural impact, and international policy aspects of this troubling and potentially dangerous disease. Each student on the team is asked to be responsible both for a specific perspective and for teaching everyone in the group the material in his or her section. Bristow writes:

> This worked well, because I added "bonus" points for folks whose teammates did above some acceptable cutoff (such as 70 percent correct) on that material on a more general exam. So for every teammate who scored over the cutoff on the molecular biology question on the exam, the student who taught the molecular biology got a bonus point. This also worked in part because I structured in a lot of individual accountability and group interdependence. Each team was asked to report in weekly on some aspect of their part done (individually), so no one could fall too far behind [Cathy Bristow, e-mail interview with the author, Jan. 1999].

Structured Academic Controversy

One of the most exciting forms of small-group learning is structured controversy discussion. Controversies and issues on which there are differing perspectives can animate almost any class or discipline. Furthermore, they can provide students with a sense that a course or discipline can be brought to bear on a thorny, interesting, and often contemporary concern. The goal is to understand the best arguments on all sides of the issue, but the students are stimulated to prepare better arguments when they are confronted with a compelling argument from the other side.

In a structured controversy, students working in groups of two to six are assigned a perspective on an issue and asked to prepare, present, and defend that assigned point of view. The interdependence involves a group goal of understanding all sides of the issue in order to write a group report integrating the best arguments on all sides (Johnson, Johnson, and Smith, 1997, 1986; Smith, 1984).

Tom Lord, professor of biology at Indiana University of Pennsylvania (1994, 1998a, 1998b, personal interview with the author, Jan. 1999), combines the jigsaw format just described with a structured controversy. He assigns teams of four students to pro and con sides of an issue such as, "Is nuclear power the answer to our future energy needs?" He subdivides each team into four specialties—usually biotic, abiotic, social, and economic—and asks each team member to research his or her specialty topic on the issue and then teach it to the other members of the team. Initially he had two opposing teams debate the issue with each other in a fishbowl-type format in front of the entire class, but he decided he wanted to get all the students more actively involved. Now he divides the members of the class whose issues are not being discussed that day into eight clusters of between five and seven students and sends one of the presenting students to each of the clusters. The pro and con presenters have about thirty minutes each to try to convince the group of their position. The presenters are then switched to a cluster that has not heard their side of the issue for a second thirty

Exhibit 3.1. A Jigsaw Procedure

When you have information you need to communicate to students, an alternative to lecturing is a procedure for structuring cooperative learning groups called *jigsaw*.

Task: Think of a reading assignment you will give in the near future. Divide the assignment into multiple (2–4) parts. Plan how you will use the jigsaw procedure. Script out exactly what you will say to the class using each part of the procedure. Practice talking students through their role.

Procedure: The steps for structuring a jigsaw lesson are as follows:

1. *Create cooperative groups:* Distribute a set of instructions (See "Notes to Students," below) and materials to each group. The set needs to be divisible into the number of members of the group (two, three, or four parts). Give each member one part of the set of materials.
2. Allow *preparation pairs:* Assign students the cooperative task of meeting with someone else in the class who is a member of another learning group, and who has the same section of the material, to complete two tasks:
   • Learning and becoming an expert on the material
   • Planning how to teach the material to the other members of the group
3. Allow *practice pairs:* Assign students the cooperative task of meeting with someone else in the class who is a member of another learning group who has learned the same material to share ideas about how the material may best be taught. These practice pairs review what each plans to teach their group and how. The best ideas of both are incorporated into each presentation.
4. Create *cooperative groups:* Assign students the cooperative tasks of
   • Teaching their area of expertise to the other group members
   • Learning the material being taught by the other members
5. *Evaluate:* Assess students' degree of mastery of all the material. Recognize those groups in which all members reach the preset criterion of excellence.

Notes to Students

For this session we will use a procedure for structuring learning groups called *jigsaw*. Each member will be given a different section of the material to be learned. Each member is dependent on the others for success in learning all the material. Each member is accountable for teaching his or her material to the others and learning the material they are teaching. The *purposes* of the jigsaw procedure are as follows:

1. To provide an alternative method of introducing new material besides reading and lecture
2. To create information interdependence among members to increase their sense of mutuality
3. To ensure that participants orally rehearse and cognitively process the information being learned
4. To provide an example of high-performance teamwork

Cooperative Group

Your *task* in this group is to learn all the assigned material. Make sure each member has a different section and that all sections are covered. Work *cooperatively* to ensure that all group members master all the assigned material.

Preparation to Teach in Pairs

Take one section of the material; then find a member of another group who has the same section of the material as you do. Work cooperatively to complete these tasks:

1. *Learn and become an expert in your material.* Read the material together, discuss it, and master it. Use an active reading strategy (such as *pair reading*):
   a. Scan section headings to get an overview of the material.
   b. Silently read a paragraph (or short section).
   c. Person A summarizes the content to Person B. Person B listens, checks for accuracy, and states how it relates to material previously learned.
   d. Reverse roles, and repeat the procedure.
2. *Plan how to teach your material to the other group members.* Share your ideas about how best to teach the material. Make sure your partner is ready.
   a. As you read the material, underline the important points, write questions or ideas in the margins, and add our own thoughts and suggestions.
   b. When finished, write down the major ideas and supporting details or examples.
   c. Prepare one or more visual aids to help explain the material.
   d. Plan how to make the other members of your group intellectually active rather than passive while they listen to your presentation.

Practice and Consulting Pairs

If you finish the preparation and have time, meet with another person from a different group who is ready and who also prepared the same section of the material as you did. Work cooperatively to complete these tasks:

1. Review what each person plans to teach his or her group and share ideas about how to teach the material. Incorporate the best ideas from both plans into each person's presentation.
2. Make sure the other person is ready to teach the material.

Teaching and Learning Group

Meet with your original group and complete the cooperative task of ensuring that all members have mastered all the assigned material by:

1. Teaching your area of expertise to the other group members
2. Learning the material being taught by the other group members

The *presenter* should encourage:

1. Oral rehearsal
2. Elaboration and integration
3. Implementation ideas

The *listening members* should:

1. Clarify the material by asking appropriate questions
2. Help the presenter by coming up with novel ways of remembering the important ideas or facts and think creatively about the material being presented
3. Relate (out loud) the information to previous learned knowledge and elaborate on the information being presented
4. Plan (out loud) how the information can be applied in the immediate future

Exhibit 3.1. A Jigsaw Procedure *(continued)*

Monitoring the Group Work
    Collect some data about the functioning of the group to aid in later group processing. The instructor will also monitor and collect data about the material being learned and the functioning of the groups.

Evaluation and Processing
    The instructor may assess participants' mastery of all the material by giving every participant an exam or randomly calling on individuals to explain the material they learned.
    The instructor will ask each group to process briefly—for example, by asking the group to identify at least one thing that each member did to help the others learn and at least three actions that could be added to improve their learning next time.

Reminder
    Learning material in a jigsaw is not a substitute for reading the material on your own later, just as listening to a lecture is not a substitute for doing individual work. The purpose of the jigsaw is to get you involved in the material, to give you an overview, and to try to motivate you to learn more on your own.

Source: Adapted from Johnson, Johnson, and Smith, 1991.

---

minutes. Afterward, the clusters decide who they think did the better job. Lord devotes six class periods during the semester to the structured controversy. He writes:

> The students really do a good job researching their issue. I use this experience still further! At the end of the semester, each group hands in a twenty-to twenty-four-page term paper summarizing its findings. The term paper has four sections to it, one for each student's aspect (biotic, abiotic, social, and economic). I tell the students that the entire term paper must flow together, have a common format, not have repeated information in it, and share a bibliography and a resource appendix. In order not to lose points on the term paper, a team will plan the paper ahead of time and even proofread each other's entries. . . . This peer review and peer writing improves the overall quality of the paper—and gives me twelve or thirteen first-class papers to read rather than forty-eight to fifty-two term papers of different qualities.

Base Groups

Beyond active involvement with course material, a sense of belonging is one of the most important conditions that can be created in a college classroom (Astin, 1993; Palmer, 1998; Seymour and Hewitt, 1997; Tinto, 1993). Being a part of a group not only promotes academic development but also enhances personal development and increases satisfaction. A relatively simple and straightforward way to start building a supportive community is through cooperative base groups.

Base groups are long-term, heterogeneous cooperative learning groups with stable membership whose primary responsibility is to provide each student the support, encouragement, and assistance he or she needs to make academic progress (Johnson, Johnson, and Smith, 1991, 1998a). Like many formal cooperative learning groups, they are intentionally formed by the faculty member, usually after collecting information from the students. Because they often stay the same during the entire course (and occasionally even beyond it), base groups can personalize the work required and the course learning experiences. When base groups complete and submit work in group folders, the paperwork burden for the faculty member is often much reduced. Like other formal groups, base group members must be carefully chosen (usually by the instructor after collecting information on preferences, available meeting times, and many other factors), monitored (the instructor observes their conversations and interactions and gives written feedback), and often coached to improve their communication and functioning as a group.

Base groups are used by several of the educators interviewed for this chapter: Cathy Bristow, Tom Lord, Steve Richardson, and Johanna Seibt. They all have their base groups stay together for the entire term, and they stress to their students the importance of helping one another to be successful. Several use the group folder format to help manage the paperwork during class time. In addition to using base groups for breaking the ice, providing support, and managing paperwork, Cathy Bristow incorporates an intriguing idea: a weekly base-group quiz. The quiz consists of a place for students' names (to give them credit for showing up) and typical multiple-choice exam questions (five or so), each with a space below to describe why the particular answer was chosen. Bristow says it is quite easy for her to review the exams because of the smaller number and higher quality; furthermore, the responses reflect deeper understanding (Cathy Bristow, personal interview with the author, Jan. 1999).

Problem-Based Learning

Problem-based learning (PBL) is a rapidly evolving strategy for developing student learning through the process of working toward the understanding or resolution of a problem. In PBL settings, the problem is encountered *first* in the learning process (Barrows and Tamblyn, 1980). PBL is generally built around the following features: problems are the organizing focus and stimulus for learning and the vehicle for the development of problem-solving skills; new information is acquired through self-directed learning; learning is student-centered and occurs in small student groups; and teachers act as facilitators or guides (Wilkerson and Gijselaers, 1996).

One leader in problem-based learning, Barbara Duch of the University of Delaware, succinctly gives her rationale for employing PBL: "'How can I get my students to think?' is a question asked by many faculty, regardless of their disciplines. Problem-based learning is an instructional method that challenges students to 'learn to learn,' working cooperatively in groups to seek solutions to real-world problems. These problems are used to engage students' curiosity and initiate learning the subject matter. PBL prepares students to think critically and analytically, and to find and use appropriate learning resources" (Barbara Duch, personal interview with the author, June 1999).

The most impressive implementations of PBL in large-class introductory courses is occurring at Samford University in Birmingham, Alabama, and the University of Delaware in Newark. Both schools have invested heavily in faculty development and are now becoming resources to other campuses around the country.

Faculty members at the University of Delaware have implemented PBL in many introductory courses, including biology, biochemistry, chemistry, criminal justice, education, international relations, marine studies, mathematics, nutrition-dietetics, physics, political science, and exercise science (Allen, Duch, and Groh, 1996; Groh, Williams, Allen, Duch, Mierson, and White, 1997). They started with grant support from the National Science Foundation (NSF-DUE) and the Fund for Improvement of Postsecondary Education (FIPSE) and have now had more than 25 percent of the faculty participate in weeklong formal workshops.

General PBL problems and sample problems from biology, chemistry-biochemistry, criminal justice, and physics are available on their Web site (http://www.udel.edu/pbl/problems/). Exhibit 3.2 shows the first page of a problem Barbara Duch uses in a general physics class with over one hundred students.

Confronted with just this introductory information, students set to work in small groups to formulate questions and discuss what information they need to collect and how they will gather it. What is notable about this PBL approach is that students work in stages; they start by assessing what they do know (stage one), then, more important, assessing what they do not know (stage 2), then determining what they need to learn (step 3) in order to attack the problem. Duch and the recitation TAs (including peer facilitators) monitor the groups, and after they have recorded questions at each stage, she randomly samples their ideas. Each problem is set up so that once students have asked questions and produced answers at each stage, they get additional information and move to a higher level of complexity (the next stage) (Barbara Duch, personal interview with the author, June 1999).

Deborah Allen, professor of biology, University of Delaware, acknowledges the enormous commitment of time, energy, and training that was involved in transforming her introductory biology courses to a PBL format. She writes her own problems and involves a cadre of well-trained undergraduate peer tutors. A course in tutorial methods of instruction, which she developed and teaches with a colleague (Harold White, professor of chemistry and biochemistry), helps prepare these and other peer tutors in large

Exhibit 3.2. A Day in the Life of John Henry, a Traffic Cop

At 13:20 on the last Friday in September 1989 a frantic call was received at the local police station. There had been a serious automobile accident at the intersection of Main Street and State Street, with injuries involved. Lt. John Henry arrived at the scene 10 minutes after the phone call and found that two cars had collided at the intersection. In one car, the driver was unconscious and in the other car both driver and one passenger were injured.

After the emergency vehicles transported the injured to the hospital, Lt. Henry's responsibility is to investigate the accident in order to determine whether one of the drivers (or both) are responsible. With the severity of injury in this accident, the investigation is critical because there may be a fatality involved.

What questions does John Henry have to answer in this investigation? What measurements does he need to take? What data should he collect? What other information does he need to record in order to aid the investigation? What physics principles will John Henry need to use in order to help analyze the data and answer his questions?

If two cars moving at right angles to each other collide, in what direction do you expect the cars to be moving after the collision? What factors will influence the direction and distance traveled after impact?

Source: Written by Barbara Duch, 1993. Revised 1995.

---

classes across the campus for this challenging role. She reports that she enjoys teaching more than ever (a common comment among the interviewees) and goes on to say:

> I prepare well for each class—script it out much as I would prepare for facilitating a teaching workshop for faculty—but like never quite being sure what will actually happen in the classroom. Students often turn my plans upside down, and usually it works out for the better. I like the fact that students are continually teaching more about the problems I've written. I can incorporate a whole new set of goals for student learning that would not have been realistic for the way I was doing things before. The classroom is a much more relaxed and user-friendly one from my perspective as well as that of the students. I prefer the role of experienced scholar in a community of scholars much more than that of the keeper of the right answer. I'd never go back to using a traditional format [Deborah Allen, personal interview with the author, Feb. 1999].

Two of Allen's problems are available on the University of Delaware PBL Web site noted earlier: a human genetics problem entitled "When Twins Marry Twins" and an approach to addressing global warming entitled "The Geritol Solution and Twenty-Five."

Allen stresses that preparation is extraordinarily important when sharing the intellectual work space with students in a problem-based learning environment. One part of the preparation is selecting or creating problems and another is choosing the procedure to use. Duch and Allen and their colleagues have written many problems for use in their introductory science courses, and they have spent a lot of time thinking and talking about what characterizes "good problems." Their thinking is summarized on the Delaware PBL Web site mentioned earlier.

The role of the instructor is as crucial to the success of problem-based learning as it is in structured academic controversy and jigsaw. A learning environment must be designed, set up, and maintained so that students take more responsibility for their own learning and the learning of others (Johnson, Johnson, and Smith, 1991, 1998a; Millis and Cottell, 1998). In addition to structuring the learning environment and posing complex, absorbing, and muddy problems, the faculty member usually serves as a facilitator or coach. Those whose stories and insights appear above all use a formal cooperative learning format that incorporates positive interdependence (students are linked through common learning goals, single product from the group, and many other ways), individual accountability (a process to make each student responsible for learning that is operationalized by faculty randomly calling on individual students to explain his or her group's answer as well as by giving individual quizzes, exams, and written assignments), face-to-face promotive interaction (students talk through the material with one another), teamwork skills (students learn and practice communication, decision-making, conflict-management, and leadership skills), and group processing (students are given a time and structure to reflect on how well their group is working). Additional information on these five key elements as well as the instructor's role in formal cooperative learning groups is available in Johnson, Johnson, and Smith (1991, 1998a; Smith, 1995, 1996). A typical problem-based cooperative learning format is shown in Exhibit 3.3. (See Chapter Six for details.)

Duch and Allen have written extensively on the procedures, results, and cautions of the University of Delaware project, and they offer worth-

Exhibit 3.3. Problem-Based Cooperative Learning Format

Task:	To solve the problem, accomplish the task.
Individual:	To estimate answer, note strategy.
Cooperative:	To provide one set of answers from the group, strive for agreement, make sure everyone is able to explain the strategies used to solve each problem.
Expected criteria for success:	Everyone must be able to explain the strategies used to solve each problem.
Evaluation:	Best answer within available resources or constraints.
Individual accountability:	One member from any group may be randomly chosen (a) to explain the answer and (b) to explain how to solve each problem.
Expected behaviors:	Active participating, checking, encouraging, and elaborating by all members.
Intergroup cooperation:	Whenever it is helpful, check procedures, answers, and strategies.

while advice for any instructor considering using of PBL with a small group. Readers are strongly urged to go to this literature for a more thorough understanding of the PBL process. Also, extensive evidence is available documenting the effectiveness of formal cooperative learning (Johnson, Johnson, and Smith, 1991, 1998b; Springer, Stanne, and Donovan, 1999).

Restructured Lecture-Recitation-Laboratory

Several faculty have become so committed to small-group learning that they have moved to redesign their large classes completely to foster it. Three examples involving large-enrollment classes are described here: chemistry at the University of Wisconsin-Madison, physics at the University of Minnesota, and the ModularCHEM Consortium at the University of Calfornia-Berkeley.

John Wright, professor of chemistry at the University of Wisconsin-Madison, teaches five different courses, including Chem 110, which has 120 students in each section. He reports, "I'd always been frustrated because of the really good students, the A-level students who always get the test questions right. When I would talk with these students about something practical, they often could not connect to an application" (John Wright, personal interview with the author, Oct. 1998).

Wright provides a lot of variety during his class sessions. Sometimes he lectures; other times he structures total involvement on the part of the students. For example, he often assigns different rows different conditions for a problem and the different rows have to come up with answers. Students' schedules are arranged so that each lab section and quiz section has the same group of students and same TA. Wright concedes that having the students stay together "takes some logistical organizing but it is the only way to go" (John Wright, personal interview with the author, Oct. 1998).

Wright establishes a student board of directors, a group of six to fifteen students who meet with him once a week for twenty minutes to provide feedback on the course. This is similar to Ed Nuhfer's student management teams approach (Nuhfer, 1997). Wright says, "This weekly feedback is one of the really important things I do, especially when I am trying new methods in the class. I am trying to walk the fine line in group learning where the problems are tough enough to make students want to work in groups but not so tough that students get frustrated. I truly value the weekly feedback from the board of directors. There have been times when I've walked into the board meeting really trembling, because I do push to the edge of students' capabilities" (John Wright, personal interview with the author, Oct. 1998).

Wright and colleagues (Millar, Kosciuk, Penberthy, and Wright, 1996; Wright, Millar, Kosciuk, Penberthy, Williams, and Wampold, 1998) documented the effects of cooperative learning in a fascinating study comparing Chem 110 taught by a highly experienced faculty member using a lecture-centered approach (response lecturing, or RL) with one taught by a cooperatively structured approach (structured active learning, or SAL). Randomly selected students from each section were examined individually and orally by about three of twenty-five faculty from chemistry and related disciplines. Students in the SAL section outperformed students in the RL section in all subcategories—analogy, analysis, meta-awareness, and agility—with the largest difference in the meta-awareness subgroup.

The University of Minnesota (collaborative) model for large introductory courses, headed by Patricia and Ken Heller, is an elaborate integration of formal cooperative groups, context-rich problems, and a detailed and explicit problem-solving strategy that is developed throughout the course (Heller, 1999). The introductory physics course has five different lecture sections, each taught by a different lecturer. The lecture sections vary in size from about 150 to 300, totaling about 900 students per quarter. All lecture sections use the cooperative group structure for laboratories and discussion sections. The formal three-member groups (assigned by the teaching assistant for that laboratory or discussion section) work together during the discussion section and laboratory. Informal, self-chosen groups participate in informal activities during the lecture. Formal roles—manager, recorder-checker, skeptic, and energizer-summarizer (if there is a four-person group)—are assigned and rotated. Students spend the most of their time clarifying and solving physics problems working in groups, guided by the course manual, *The Competent Problem Solver: A Strategy for Solving Problems in Physics* (Keith, Heller, and Heller).

The course Web site provides a comprehensive look at the educators' approach to helping students learn physics. They summarize, for example, their implementation of the cognitive apprenticeship approach (modeling, coaching and scaffolding, fading) for helping students participate in the "culture of expert practice"—an environment in which teachers and students not only are engaged in solving problems but also are actively communicating about them with fellow students and teachers. Ken Heller sums up the shift to cooperative learning as follows: "Individual performance on problem solving is one of the reasons we went to cooperative learning. That cooperative groups are effective for individual learning is something that many people don't appreciate" (Ken Heller, personal interview with the author, Mar. 1999). Further details on the Hellers' approach is available in several systematic studies (Heller, Keith, and Anderson, 1992; Heller and Hollabaugh, 1992).

The large-scale experimentation taking place in the ModularCHEM Consortium in chemistry is similar to the Minnesota and Wisconsin models in that the lecture format continues to be used but major renovations have been made to the discussion sections. Funded by the National Science Foundation, the ModularCHEM Consortium is developing and evaluating a modular approach to teaching chemistry. The project has developed several evaluation instruments to help assess the effectiveness of their materials. The evaluation forms are available on the project Web site (mc2.cchem .berkeley.edu).

Eliminated Lecture, Substitution of Hands-On Laboratory

Michigan State University's introductory nonmajor computer science course CSE 101 is taken by about four thousand students each year. Until recently it was taught in classes of fifty to sixty, with students viewing tapes of faculty teaching computer science. Mark Urban-Lurain, instructor in the Department of Computer Science and Engineering at Michigan State, said that they put everything they knew how to do into the tapes (professional studio quality, great graphics and animations, careful scripts) but that students did not learn the material in these presentations. In fact, students not only performed poorly on laboratory exercises covering the lecture materials but also had poor retention of concepts (Mark Urban-Lurain, personal interview with the author, Jan. 1999).

Don Weinshank, professor of computer science at Michigan State University, and Urban-Lurain volunteered to redesign the course completely. They started by surveying of all departments that required the course, asking, among other things, "What would you like students who are successful in the course to be able to do?" They then developed a core sequence with three follow on tracks (general, spreadsheets for data analysis, and spreadsheets for fiscal analysis).

Now, at the beginning of each two-hour class period, students sign in and are assigned a partner for the day. The classes of thirty students are facilitated by a lead graduate teaching assistant, who is assisted by an undergraduate TA. The two-hour laboratory sessions, which meet twice each week, are scripted in great detail because sixty laboratory sessions go on each week. For example, the TAs' script for day twenty of the general track on "Designing a Web Site" is ten pages long. At the beginning of the term, tasks have five- and ten-minute limits; toward the end, the tasks become more complex and last twenty minutes or more.

In their course redesign, Weinshank and Urban-Lurain implemented a modified mastery evaluation system. In this model, bridge task tests are administered in each laboratory section once each week. They are computer-generated, unique for each student, and administered by a TA who is different from the one teaching the section. They are graded pass or fail, and students must pass each successive bridge task before being permitted to take the next one. Or they may stop and take the grade they have currently earned. Because bridge task tests are given only twelve times during the semester, some students exhaust their opportunities for a higher grade. Students may earn a grade as high as 3.0 by passing the bridge tasks. To earn a 3.5 or 4.0, students must complete an individual project that integrates their earlier learning.

One of the great surprises for these teachers was the grade distribution. The average GPA for the course has consistently been at about 3.0, and the distributions are skewed to the right. Weinshank and Urban-Lurain worried about this until they explored the literature and found this quote from Bloom, Madaus, and Hastings (1981): "If we are effective in our instruction, the distribution of achievement should be very different from the normal curve. In fact, we may even insist that our educational efforts have been unsuccessful to the extent that the distribution of achievements approximates the normal distribution" (p. 52).

Weinshank and Urban-Lurain designed a tightly integrated system where textbooks are custom-published, laboratories are carefully and thoroughly designed, TAs are well trained, and everything works together. They try to be as authentic as possible by using realistic problems and tasks and having students work in teams. Several papers describe their work (Urban-Lurain and Weinshank, 1999a, 1999b, 1999c), and the CSE 101 Web site is very thorough (www.cse.msu.edu/~cse101).

Constructivist Pedagogy

Several faculty members with whom we spoke (Allen, Duch, Dykstra, Lord, Urban-Lurain, and Weinshank) talked about their understanding of and commitment to the notion of constructivism. Some have referred to it in their published work (Dykstra, 1996; Lord, 1994; Urban-Lurain and Weinshank, 1999c). According to Catherine Fosnot (1996), constructivism is not a theory about teaching but rather a theory about knowledge and learning. The theory defines knowledge as temporary, developmental, and socially and culturally mediated, and thus, nonobjective. Learning from this perspective is understood as a self-regulated process of resolving inner cognitive conflicts that often become apparent through concrete experience, collaborative discourse, and reflection.

As is no doubt now clear, the faculty members interviewed for this chapter—whether or not they are conversant with the literature on the subject—are practicing elements of constructivist pedagogy. They are trying multiple things at once, inside and outside the classroom. They are exploring different ways of conceiving courses to engage students, facilitate problem solving, build critical-thinking and reasoning skills, and create community. Once faculty members start treating students as emerging scholars and developing professionals, and once they open up the classroom to student-student interaction, they discover endless opportunities for sharing the intellectual feast. Involving students in these more engaging (and time-consuming) activities is a challenge for many educators, given the lecture-centered tradition that is so firmly entrenched in college and university teaching. But as the examples described in this chapter indicate, doing this is not only possible, it is happening!

References

Allen, D. E., and Duch, B. J. *Thinking Toward Solutions: Problem-Based Activities for General Biology.* Philadelphia: Saunders College Publishing, 1998.

Allen, D. E., Duch, B. J., and Groh, S. E. "The Power of Problem-Based Learning in Teaching Introductory Science Courses." In L. Wilkerson and W. H. Gijselaers (eds.), *Bringing Problem-Based Learning to Higher Education: Theory and Practice.* New Directions for Teaching and Learning, no. 68. San Francisco: Jossey-Bass, 1996.

Angelo, T. A., and Cross, K. P. *Classroom Assessment Techniques: A Handbook for College Teachers.* San Francisco: Jossey-Bass, 1993.

Aronson, E. *The Jigsaw Classroom.* Thousand Oaks, Calif.: Sage, 1978.

Astin, A. *What Matters in College? Four Critical Years Revisited.* San Francisco: Jossey-Bass, 1993.

Barrows, H. S., and Tamblyn, R. *Problem-Based Learning.* New York: Springer, 1980.

Bloom, B. S., Madaus, G. F., and Hastings, J. T. *Evaluation to Improve Learning.* New York: McGraw-Hill, 1981.

Bristow, C. M. "Applications of Environmental and Organismal Biology Teaching Science as Parable." *The Scholarship of Teaching,* 1995, *1*(1), 17–24.

Christensen, C. R. *Teaching by the Case Method.* Cambridge, Mass: Harvard Business School, 1981.

Christensen, C. R., Garvin, D. A., and Sweet, A. *Education for Judgment: The Artistry of Discussion Leadership.* Cambridge, Mass.: Harvard Business School, 1991.

Duch, B. J. "Problem-Based Learning in Physics: The Power of Students Teaching Students." *About Teaching,* Jan. 1995, 47.

Dykstra, D. I., Jr. "Teaching Introductory Physics to College Students." In Fosnot, C. T. (ed.), *Constructivism: Theory, Perspectives, and Practice.* New York: Teachers College Press, 1996.

Dykstra, D. I., Jr., Boyle, Franklin C. and Monarch, I. A. "Studying Conceptual Change in Learning Physics." *Science Education,* 1992, 76(6), 615–652.

Ebert-May, D., Brewer, C., and Allred, S. "Innovation in Large Lectures: Teaching for Active Learning." *BioScience,* 1997, 47(9), 601–607.

Fosnot, C. T. *Enquiring Teachers, Enquiring Learners: A Constructivist Approach for Teaching.* New York: Teachers Collee Press, 1989.

Fosnot, C. T. (ed.). *Constructivism: Theory, Perspectives, and Practice.* New York: Teachers College Press, 1996.

Groh, S. E., Williams, B. A., Allen, D. E., Duch, B. J., Mierson, S., and White, H. B. "Institutional Change in Science Education: A Case Study." In A. P. McNeal and C. D'Avanzo (eds.), *Student Active Science: Models of Innovation in College Science Teaching.* Philadelphia: Saunders College Publishing, 1997.

Heller, K. "The University of Minnesota (Collaborative) Model for Large Introductory Courses." [www.physics.umn.edu/groups/physed]. 1999.

Heller, P., and Hollabaugh, M. "Teaching Problem Solving Through Cooperative Grouping. Part 2: Designing Problems and Structuring Groups." *American Journal of Physics,* 1992, *60*(7), 637–645.

Heller, P., Keith, R., and Anderson, S. "Teaching Problem Solving Through Cooperative Grouping. Part 1: Group Versus Individual Problem Solving." *American Journal of Physics,* 1992, *60*(7), 627–636.

Johnson, D. W., Johnson, R. T. and Smith, K. A. "Academic Conflict Among Students: Controversy and Learning." In R. Feldman (ed.), *Social Psychological Applications to Education.* Cambridge: Cambridge University Press, 1986.

Johnson, D. W., Johnson, R. T., and Smith, K. A. "Cooperative Learning: Increasing College Faculty Instructional Productivity." ASHE-ERIC Higher Education Report No. 4. Washington, D.C.: George Washington University, 1991.

Johnson, D. W., Johnson, R. T., and Smith, K. A. "Academic Controversy: Enriching College Instruction with Constructive Controversy." ASHE-ERIC Higher Education Report No. 25. Washington, D.C.: George Washington University, 1997.

Johnson, D. W., Johnson, R. T., and Smith, K. A. *Active Learning: Cooperation in the College Classroom* (2nd ed.). Edina, Minn.: Interaction Books, 1998a.

Johnson, D. W., Johnson, R. T., and Smith, K. A. "Cooperative Learning Returns to College: What Evidence Is There That It Works?" *Change,* 1998b, *30*(4), 26–35.

Kalman, J., and Kalman, C. "Writing to Learn." *American Journal of Physics,* 1996, *64,* 954–955.

Lord, T. R. "Using Constructivisim to Enhance Student Learning in College Biology." *Journal for College Science Teaching,* May 1994, pp. 346–348.

Lord, T. R. "A Comparison Between Traditional and Constructivist Teaching in College Biology." *Innovative Higher Education,* 1998a, *2*(3), 197–216.

Lord, T. R. "Cooperative Learning That Really Works in Biology Teaching." *American Biology Teacher,* 1998b, *60*(8), 580–588.

Millar, S. B., Kosciuk, S. A., Penberthy, D. L., and Wright, J. C. "Faculty Assessment of the Effects of a Freshman Chemistry Course." *Proceedings of the 1996 Annual Conference of the American Society for Engineering Education.*

Millis, B. J., and Cotell, P. G., Jr. *Cooperative Learning for Higher Education Faculty.* Phoenix: Oryx Press, 1998.

Nuhfer, E. "Student Management Teams: The Heretic's Path to Teaching Success." In W. E. Campbell and K. A. Smith (eds.), *New Paradigms for College Teaching.* Edina, Minn.: Interaction Books, 1997.

Palmer, P. *The Courage to Teach.* San Francisco: Jossey-Bass, 1998.

Seymour, E., and Hewitt, N. M. *Talking About Leaving: Why Undergraduates Leave the Sciences.* Boulder, Colo.: Westview Press, 1997.

Smith, K. A. "Structured Controversy." *Engineering Education,* 1984, *74*(5), 306–309.

Smith, K. A. "Cooperative Learning: Effective Teamwork for Engineering Classrooms." IEEE Education Society/ASEE electrical engineering division newsletter, Mar. 1995, 1–6.

Smith, K. A. "Cooperative Learning: Making 'Groupwork' Work." In C. Bonwell and T. Sutherlund (eds.), *Active Learning: Lessons from Practice and Emerging Issues.* New Directions for Teaching and Learning, no. 67. San Francisco: Jossey-Bass, 1996.

Springer, L., Stanne, M. E., and Donovan, S. "Effects of Small-Group Learning on Undergraduates in Science, Mathematics, Engineering, and Technology: A Meta-Analysis." *Review of Educational Research,* 1999, *69*(1), 50–80.

Tinto, V. *Leaving College: Rethinking the Causes and Cures of Student Attrition* (2nd ed.). Chicago: University of Chicago Press, 1993.

Urban-Lurain, M., and Weinshank, D. "Vignette: Computing Concepts and Competencies." *Computer-Enhanced Learning: 100 Courses at 50 of America's Most Wired Colleges.* Winston-Salem, N.C.: International Center for Computer Enhanced Learning, Wake Forest University, Jan. 7–10, 1999a.

Urban-Lurain, M., and Weinshank, D. "I Do and I Understand: Mastery Model for a Large Nonmajor Course." SIGSCE (Special Interest Group, Computer Science Education). Annual meeting of the Association for Computer Machinery, New Orleans, March 1999b.

Urban-Lurain, M., and Weinshank, D. "Mastering Computing Technology: A New Approach for Noncomputer Science Majors." AERA 99, Division C, Section 7; American Educational Research Association, Montreal, April 1999c.

Wilkerson, L., and Gijselaers, W. H. (eds.). *Bringing Problem-Based Learning to Higher Education: Theory and Practice.* New Directions for Teaching and Learning, no. 68. San Francisco: Jossey-Bass, 1996.

Wright, J. C., Millar, S. B., Kosciuk, S. A., Penberthy, D. L., Williams, P. H., and Wampold, B. E. "A Novel Strategy for Assessing the Effects of Curriculum Reform on Student Competence." *Journal of Chemistry Education,* 1998, *75,* 986.

4

In a number of new initiatives, the problems of a fragmented curriculum and student isolation in existing large classes are addressed through peer-facilitated learning opportunities, or more ambitiously, by restructuring the curriculum to create linked classes.

Restructuring Large Classes to Create Communities of Learners

Jean MacGregor

A widening stream of research is identifying the power of the student peer group in enhancing student persistence, achievement, and satisfaction in undergraduate settings (Johnson and Johnson, 1989; Pascarella and Terenzini, 1991; Astin, 1993; Light, 1992; Springer, Stanne, and Donovan, 1999; Tinto, 1997). Students are increasingly telling us that engaging with other students on meaningful academic tasks makes a critical difference in their involvement in college. Yet the question remains: How can we best set up conditions for students to participate in meaningful collaborative learning activities when the very structures of undergraduate courses—not to mention the complexity of students' lives—do not foster sustained focus or opportunities to cultivate human relationships? As the authors in this volume argue, many lower-division classes are large. A significant number are huge. Furthermore, students experience classroom learning in fragments, with different groups of students in different sets of courses usually meeting for brief periods of time and having little or no relationship with each other. This multiple-course delivery structure might have been effective when it was created in the early part of the twentieth century. In those days, most students lived in residence halls and were not distracted by commuting, jobs, family responsibilities, or the constant lure of radio, television, stereos, and the Internet.

Today's prevailing course structures are problematic for faculty members too. Large class sizes and the customary sixty- or seventy-five-minute blocks of time put enormous constraints on their ability to know students, to involve them in constructing their own understanding of the course's concepts, or to ask them to demonstrate that understanding in all but the most routinized ways. Most teachers with whom we speak know this format is not effective for most students' engagement or learning, yet the political economies of our universities seem to have locked these structures in place.

In recent years, though, a number of new initiatives have emerged that live within and alongside large classes. The intentions behind them are to foster greater focus and community among students and deeper engagement with learning. Some of these programs are built around discrete courses and make effective use of student peer facilitators and community building to strengthen learning and student-completion rates. Others are curricular learning communities in the sense of "purposefully linking courses or coursework so that students find greater coherence in what they are learning as well as increased interaction with faculty and fellow students" (Gabelnick, MacGregor, Matthews, and Smith, 1990, p. 5).

Although these programs vary considerably in their structural design and strategies for small-group learning, they share intentions and elements. They create small, knowable communities of students with an academic purpose. They develop active, collaborative learning environments where understanding of course content is shared and constructed. They intentionally increase time on task through formal and informal activities related to the coursework. The collaborative activities themselves increase feedback loops among students as they test their understanding and share information, questions, and study strategies. In the multiple-course learning community models, intellectual connections are drawn between two or more classes. That these initiatives include such elements should come as no surprise to most readers of this series: they have been repeatedly promoted as keys to good practice in undergraduate education (NIE Study Group, 1984; Chickering and Gamson, 1987, 1991). This chapter will describe some of the initiatives and mention some of the challenges involved in establishing them.

Peer-Facilitated Communities

In large universities, many initiatives are working to strengthen the existing pattern of large-class offerings by creating additional meeting points or even credit-bearing courses every week to increase community, engagement, and ultimately, student success. Undergraduate peer advisers or facilitators are often the lynchpins in these initiatives. As undergraduates at the same institution, these "near peers" bring experiences and perspectives not usually shared by graduate teaching assistants, who generally experienced their undergraduate education elsewhere. In addition, for the undergraduates involved, these programs provide rare leadership opportunities, teaching responsibilities, and often a unique preprofessional development experience as well.

Supplemental Instruction Programs. Perhaps the mostly widely known and consistently evaluated approach to peer-facilitated learning is the long-standing Supplemental Instruction Program invented at University of Missouri-Kansas City in the early 1970s. This initiative took the fresh approach of targeting not high-risk students but rather high-risk classes—those distinguished by high rates of withdrawal and failure. These classes are generally characterized by "large amounts of weekly reading from both difficult textbooks and secondary library reference works, infrequent examinations that focus on higher cognitive levels of Bloom's taxonomy, voluntary and unrecorded class attendance, and large classes in which each student has little opportunity for interaction with the professor or the other students" (Martin and Arendale, 1994, pp. 11–12). Any student in the class can voluntarily participate in one or more of the three Supplemental Instruction (SI) sessions offered each week, which are convened by an SI leader—a specially trained, more advanced undergraduate student who has successfully completed the targeted class. The SI sessions stress not only the course content but also study strategies and learning and thinking strategies; SI leaders are trained to facilitate small-group discussion, rather than repeat the lectures. An important feature of this model is the collaboration between the class professor and the SI leader, who sits in on the course and often gives the professor feedback on the students' progress as well as their difficulties in understanding course material. Another important feature is that SI does not present itself to students as a remedial program but rather as an optional supplement open to all students in the class at any time. Building on the voluminous studies demonstrating the efficacy of this program, UMKC has disseminated the SI approach to literally hundreds of campuses in the United States and abroad. In any given year now, over 350 campuses are running SI programs, reaching about 250,000 students. SI pioneers Deanna Martin and David Arendale present a thorough description of this approach in the New Directions for Teaching and Learning Series volume they edited, *Supplemental Instruction: Increasing Achievement and Retention* (Martin and Arendale, 1994).

Emerging Scholars Programs. This approach parallels Supplemental Instruction in creating an academic community of students facilitated by a more advanced undergraduate peer facilitator. This strategy emerged at University of California, Berkeley, in the 1980s in mathematics, through Uri Treisman's groundbreaking and highly successful effort to increase African American students' achievement rates in the calculus sequence (Treisman, 1985, 1992; Fullilove and Treisman, 1990). The problem, Treisman found, was not deficiencies in academic skills or motivation but rather in patterns of academic isolation. His strategy: highly collaborative math skills workshops that would increase students' time on task with calculus through highly involving problems and increase student community at the same time. These skills workshops, variously called Emerging Scholars Programs (ESP), academic excellence workshops, math excel programs, or by other locally appropriate names, have now spread to well over a hundred campuses across the country and are being developed in a variety of introductory science and engineering courses in addition to those in the introductory college mathematics sequence.

Emerging Scholars Programs differ from the Supplemental Instruction approach in several ways. These programs are associated with math, engineering, and increasingly, other introductory-level science courses. Historically they targeted underrepresented minorities and women, although now at many universities the recruited participants are a purposefully heterogeneous mix of students of color and white students, and the program is marketed as an academic excellence program. At research universities, the program carries elective departmental credit and is taught by a graduate TA. At regional colleges and universities, participation is generally voluntary, but a semester-long commitment and consistent attendance is expected: students are asked to join in a formal workshop group of about seven to twelve students associated with their course for the entire term. More advanced undergraduates serve as the facilitators of these programs. Perhaps most important, the workshop pedagogy is carefully constructed around small-group problem solving and facilitated by a peer undergraduate, often a student of color who is majoring in the discipline of the course.

Several impressive evaluation studies of these programs at the University of Wisconsin (Alexander, Burda, and Millar, 1997; Kosciuk, 1997), Cal Poly-Pomona (Bonsangue and Drew, 1995; Bonsangue, 1994) and the University of Texas-Austin (Moreno, Muller, Asera, Wyatt, and Epperson, 1999) consistently demonstrate the power of this approach, with Emerging Scholars students outperforming and "outpersisting" nonparticipants.

Freshman Interest Groups. A different strategy for building community in large university settings is Freshman Interest Groups (FIGs). Jack Bennett, director of advising at the University of Oregon, invented this learning community model in 1983; since then, numbers of other large campuses have adapted FIGs, including the University of Washington, the University of Missouri-Columbia, Illinois State University, and the University of Indiana. In these programs, groups of fifteen to twenty students enroll in two, or more frequently, three courses related to a common interest or preparatory for a major. The following list provides a sample of the ninety different FIGs at the University of Washington:

Ancient culture	Community and place
Classical art and literature	Comparative history of ideas
Modern America	International relations
Human behavior	The cosmos
Culture and gender	Life science
Performing arts: dance	Physical science
Performing arts: drama	Engineering
Education	Geology

Usually one course in the mix is a small-enrollment course, such as English composition or speech communication, whereas the others are large-enrollment settings. In addition, the student groups meet at least once a week in a freshman proseminar convened by a more advanced undergraduate peer adviser. At some institutions, the peer adviser is joined by a faculty member or a student affairs professional as a cofacilitator, but generally the proseminar is the undergraduate student leader's responsibility. Some campuses have deepened the cocurricular dimension of FIGs by situating the programs and the students in residence halls, so students in a common FIG live on the same or contiguous floors along with their peer adviser. Another successful variation, at the University of Washington, is Transfer Interest Groups (TRIGs), geared to transfer students enrolling in large three-hundred-level classes that are the gateways to study in the major.

The faculty members who teach courses embedded in FIGs are not expected to teach their courses differently, although some professors report that they look for ways to illuminate the theme or emphasis of the FIG. Connections and community develop in the proseminar component of the model. FIG proseminar activities vary a great deal even within a university program, ranging from building informal and formal study groups, working on time management and study strategies, getting oriented to and enrolled in the university's electronic mail system, receiving academic advisement for subsequent terms, learning about the career paths of university alumni who majored in the interest group's discipline or professional concentration, engaging in community service projects, attending campus events together or going on a FIG-related field trip. These are just a few of the many directions a FIG can take. Through these activities, FIG programs provide students in their first term in college with an immediate and consistent community of fellow students with similar academic interests, an opportunity to meet and converse informally with the faculty members of the cluster of classes, an orientation to the university and its services, and a constellation of coherent classes. Although many faculty members of the largest classes do not know which of their students are enrolled in a Freshman Interest Group, those who do at the University of Washington have reported that their FIG students seem the most academically engaged and seem to participate in more lively discussions (Lowell, 1997).

FIGs have been so successful in helping students make the transition to college (Tokuno and Campbell, 1992; Tinto and Goodsell, 1993) that programs on some campuses now reach very large numbers of students: 45 percent of the freshman class at University of Washington now enroll in ninety FIGs, and plans are afoot to scale up the program to 60 percent of the class by fall 2000. Similarly, University of Missouri's FIG program (based in residence halls), which served about 25 percent of its freshman class in 1999, has also generated positive response from students and significantly increased student retention (Pike, Schroeder, and Berry, 1996; Schroeder and Hurst, 1996). At this same institution, a residential "House Environment Survey" comparing students enrolled in FIG programs with those not enrolled in fall 1997 revealed that FIG students were generally more engaged in both the academic and residential communities than their non-FIG student peers. The most dramatic difference was that FIG students reported that they regularly got together in the dorms for study sessions (Johnson, 1998).

Linked Freshman Seminars. Hundreds of campuses have developed small freshman-orientation courses to ease the transition from high school to college and to build student confidence in navigating the university setting. These classes vary greatly in staffing and content. Although some of these freshman seminars (also called University 101 or Freshman Year Experience classes) focus on study skills and other basic strategies for student success, others are more centered on content and on learning how to learn in a specific discipline.

Washington State University's freshman seminars have gone in a different direction: they use electronic technology, the academic content of a class, and collaborative learning to ask—and find answers to—academic questions. Freshman seminars at this institution are elective, two-credit offerings, again taught by undergraduate peer facilitators. A team of graduate students supervise the peer facilitators (at a ratio of about 1:5) and act as the faculty of record for the seminars, which are offered on a pass-fail basis. Each of the forty-five seminar sections (reaching about a quarter of WSU's freshman class) is attached to a large general education course, most often the university's required class in world civilization but also such introductory courses as political science, biological science, communications, sociology, anthropology, and geology. Some of these classes are medium enrollment (eighty to one hundred students) whereas others are much higher (two hundred to four hundred students). In the seminar, students meet in one of three classrooms specially designed for technology use and collaborative learning, and they receive and submit their weekly homework assignments on-line. They learn library and Internet research skills while at the same time how to ask questions appropriate to the discipline or specific content of the course they are taking together. The faculty members of the linked class get involved with coaching both the peer facilitator and the seminar participants, and giving feedback on the research questions. Research librarians also act as resources to every seminar group. The semester culminates in a big public celebration: a large poster session and multimedia fair mounted by all the seminars and attended by faculty and staff, university leadership, and local media. Jean Henscheid, formerly the coordinator of freshman programs for WSU's Student Advising and Learning Center and now associate director of the National Resource Center for the First-Year Experience and Students in Transition at University of South Carolina, reports that students in the seminars "seem to perform better on problem solving, critical thinking, analyzing a situation, asking for help, understanding the content of the linked course, and accepting and tolerating different points of view. Our data indicate that the freshman seminar students generally outperform their peers in the same lecture class, but the most dramatic gains are for the students whose intake profiles are at the lower end" (Jean Henscheid, personal interview with the author, Dec. 1998).

Linked Class Learning Communities

In curricular learning communities, faculty members come more centrally into the picture as creators of social connections among students and intellectual connections among classes. In large university settings, the linked-class arrangement most often takes the form of a small-enrollment class being attached to a larger one.

Wraparound Seminars. For the past several years, Monica Devanas has been teaching Biomedical Issues of HIV/AIDS, the highest enrollment single-sectioned class (about 400 to 450 students) at Rutgers University that meets general education distribution requirements for sciences. In addition to creating a lively science class through a compelling and timely subject, the use of a technology-equipped "smart" classroom, occasional short turn-to-your-neighbor discussion activities in class, lots of guest presenters, and an option for students to gain extra credit through participation in one of many on-line discussion groups tied to the course, Devanas has established the option for students to enroll in one or more credit-bearing minicourses known as wraparound seminars. So in addition to studying the microbiology and epidemiology of AIDS, theories of infection, human immune system responses, and new research directions, students have the option of taking a credited course in any of a dozen disciplines, which extends their understanding of the disease into the social sciences or humanities. In recent years, wraparound seminars have included study in education, criminal justice, Africana studies, communications, English, human ecology, journalism, psychology, urban studies, and women's studies. The political science department has incorporated the wraparound into HIV and Public Policy, a permanent three-credit course in the curriculum with an optional service-learning component, which students can take simultaneously with the HIV/AIDS course or before or after it.

Although Devanas has recruited some tenure-track faculty to teach a seminar, it has been more generally the case that the wraparounds have been taught by nontenured instructors or graduate TAs, usually doctoral students with research interests in HIV/AIDS. She compensates these wraparound hosts with small honoraria—"budget dust," as she calls it—from the health education office on the campus. The seminars are generally small enrollment (fifteen to thirty students) and research- or project-oriented, creating little communities of interest and exploration within the larger HIV/AIDS class and an "enriched understanding of the relatedness of the disciplinary issues with the scientific knowledge to date, and the importance of psychosocial issues in global health crises" (Monica Devanas, personal interview with the author, Jan. 1999). Evaluations of the wraparound seminars reveal that students who elect to take them have higher motivation for and gain higher grades in the large class.

Linked Writing Courses. From both inside and outside the academy we hear constant clarion calls for college graduates to be better writers. The past two decades have seen flurries of commitment to engage faculty and departments in "writing across the curriculum" efforts, so that students write more during their undergraduate careers and take writing more seriously in a range of courses. These WAC programs have spawned writing-intensive courses in the disciplines and in general education classes, as well as faculty development efforts geared toward enabling teachers to develop and respond to writing assignments in their specific classes. In recent years, some campuses have moved to incorporate writing competency tests or writing portfolios in their general education requirements. Still, most faculty outside English or journalism departments find it a challenging proposition to include writing in their courses, especially as enrollments grow.

In these same decades, another kind of WAC effort has been quietly emerging—writing in the disciplines, or WID. One major WID strategy involves linking writing courses to large general education lecture courses. Generally, one or more small subsets of students in a general education class simultaneously enroll in a writing class whose reading and writing work relates directly to the content of the larger class. The writing instructor and the lecture-course faculty member often collaborate on the development of the writing assignments and help students explore what it means to write in the discipline. These writing links can be found at any number of two- and four-year colleges, but two universities have mounted substantial writing-link programs specifically to give depth and content to required composition courses, to strengthen learning in large lecture courses, and to advance writing in the disciplines.

The University of Washington's Interdisciplinary Writing Program (or IWP) has been in place since 1977. Sixty-five linked writing classes are offered each year, reaching about thirteen hundred students. Most of the links are to large general education courses such as political science, psychology, history of art, history, sociology, geography, international studies, and philosophy, although a few are linked to large-enrollment junior-level classes, such as Modern Political Theory and Developmental Psychology. Each year during fall term, almost all writing links are included in the university's Freshman Interest Group program (described previously), creating an even more academically coherent experience for freshmen.

George Mason University began offering linked writing courses in 1986, and like the University of Washington, mounts a significant number of writing links (twenty-five to thirty-five) each year to social science and humanities courses and occasionally to biology and geology classes as well. At both institutions, there are frequently two linked writing sections in a large lecture class.

The teaching opportunities in a writing link are affected by the nature of the accompanying lecture course and the kind of collaboration between the lecture-course teacher and the writing-course teacher. Some lecture courses are surveys in the most fragmented sense, and a writing teacher whose class is linked to such a survey must do much more independent work to define good writing tasks, to capture and deepen what is going by so fast in the lecture. Both the University of Washington and George Mason University work to identify lecture courses that build in an element of inquiry and conceptual tension even when enrollments are large. As Joan Graham, director of the IWP at UW puts it, "We seek out lectures that focus on questions, perhaps introducing students to the consequences of different theories, or modeling ways of evaluating different kinds of evidence. Writing assignments in such contexts are especially productive, and writing links carry students much further into lecture course issues and readings than they are otherwise likely to go. We often give students so much rich material and ask them to do so little with it! It is a constant irony" (Joan Graham, personal interview with the author, Oct. 1998).

At both institutions, the linked writing classes ask students to do a lot with the material. They require reading and research assignments that extend the content of the lecture class, and writing assignments to build connections and help students develop questions of their own. Peer writing groups are at the heart of the pedagogy of these classes. Linked writing students approach writing as a process of thinking, drafting, getting feedback, and redrafting: "We are studying our own writing and each other's," as Graham puts it. Students who enroll in these linked classes recognize that they are more demanding than stand-alone composition courses but point to the academic community and academic connections as key to their learning (Tinto and Goodsell, 1993). Professors teaching linked classes note that students naturally form study groups, engage in course-related conversations on their own, often exhibit better and more punctual attendance, and in many instances appear to be more capable of handling more complex ideas (George Mason University, 1996).

Course-Cluster Learning Communities

These learning community models restructure students' academic experiences further than the other models by creating larger arrangements of time and space for students to learn together. Course-cluster programs package three and even four classes to be taken simultaneously by a cohort of students. Most of these programs are targeted to entering students to provide a positive transition to university learning as well as a coherent general education experience. Some of these programs have worked entirely within the normal course-loading structures of the institution; others have made enrollment changes in some courses.

The Freshman Year Initiative at CUNY-Queens College. Queens College of the City University of New York is an urban commuter school where freshmen have historically been invisible in large-lecture course environments. The only small classes they might take as beginning students are math and composition courses, often taught by adjunct faculty not deeply connected to the school. "Until the Freshman Year Initiative," writes Judith Summerfield, the program's director, "faculty had no sense of who the freshmen were, nor did the freshmen themselves. We wanted to create a freshman year—and a freshman culture. Our goal is to provide students with a coherent first year through a first semester in an academic community, where classes are taught by faculty (mostly full-timers) who have chosen to teach in the program" (Summerfield, 1998, p. 1). Queens now enrolls two-thirds of its freshman class (about six hundred students) in fourteen "academic communities" that cluster three classes: College English and two other classes. Figure 4.1 shows a typical Freshman Year Initiative cluster of courses at Queens College. Two sections of freshman composition join together for an introductory philosophy class, and this group of forty is a subset of a large sociology class.

Undergraduate teaching assistants, often Freshman Year Initiative (FYI) alumni, act as peer facilitators in the composition classes and sometimes in other classes as well. The program has been particularly successful in recruiting experienced, talented faculty genuinely interested in teaching this generation of freshmen. These teachers also welcome the dialogue with their cluster partners about their common students and teaching and learning issues. The FYI program has developed several informal but vitally important venues for community building: *Arkam* (a play on the fictional asylum in Batman comics), a room near the FYI office that is now the informal gathering and studying place for FYI-enrolled students; *ceilidhs* (a Celtic term for a story-telling and song-filled gathering), which are special events several times a semester for each community; and even a special FYI literary magazine. By all accounts, the program's reputation for good teaching and community building has over a short span of years succeeded in creating the positive freshman culture its creators envisioned.

Figure 4.1. Sample Community Structure in a Three-Course Block at CUNY-Queens College

English 110 20 Students "Dedicated Course"	English 110 20 Students "Dedicated Course"
Philosophy 101 "Dedicated Course" 40 Students	
Sociology 180 Students Total 40 FYI Students	

Triads at Texas A&M University-Corpus Christi. An upper-division and graduate school, Texas A&M-Corpus Chrsti began to plan in the early 1990s to "grow down" and enroll freshmen and sophomores in 1994. Intense planning for the needs of lower-division students and for a coherent general education experience for them resulted in an ambitious course-clustering program. In their first two semesters, all freshmen would enroll in groups of about two hundred in a "triad" of courses: two large-lecture classes that contained all of them and one of eight sections of English composition. Each composition section also met in a freshman seminar course that was convened by a graduate teaching assistant who also served as a grader in one of the large-lecture classes.

Figure 4.2 illustrates one of the triad offerings today, which generally carry ten to eleven semester credit hours. Two hundred students enroll in a political science course in American government and a related American history class. They subdivide into eight groups of about twenty-five, with each group taking a freshman composition course and a freshman seminar together.

The faculty members handling the lecture sections work to develop "touch points," major points of intersection (or opposition) between their classes. The English composition instructors (a mix of tenured faculty, part-time instructors, and graduate teaching assistants) work collaboratively to create writing assignments related to the triad themes and teach all the writing classes in computer labs. To prepare to teach in this complex model, the graduate students involved in both the writing courses and the freshman seminars participate in an intensive summer institute prior to each academic year—an impressive commitment to the training and professional development of both teaching assistants and faculty. The triads program now serves about seven hundred incoming freshmen every year; they fulfill twenty to

Figure 4.2. Triad Cluster at Texas A&M University-Corpus Christi

A general education lecture class: Introduction to American Government (200 students)
A general education lecture class: U.S. History (200 students)
These 200 are then divided into 8 sections (25 each) of English Composition and a Freshman Seminar, led by a graduate TA who also serves as a grader in one of the general education classes.

twenty-one semester credits, or about 40 percent of the university's core curriculum requirements.

Several other campuses have put large cluster programs in place: Temple University in Philadelphia, University of Northern Colorado, Ball State University, and University of Texas, El Paso. UTEP's program is notable because the clusters are built as the intake ports for all students interested in majoring in engineering, mathematics, or the sciences, and in those clusters faculty are making substantial commitments to cooperative learning across all their classes. Clusters are developmentally tiered to serve both college-ready and underprepared students. Clusters like these can be powerful for students in making the large-university environment seem small. Indeed, many students comment that the real value of these programs is "being in small classes," even though they are still enrolled in some very large ones.

However, clustering courses is not without organizational challenges. These programs have the most impact on students when commitments are made to take seriously the building of community and to form some deliberate intellectual "glue" among the classes. Merely grouping the students in block registration cohorts may enable them to see each other in class, but if no effort is made to build community or take advantage of the learning possibilities that the related courses invite, the learning and the community remain in the shallows. Because many cluster programs include freshman-level composition or mathematics classes staffed by graduate teaching assistants, learning community program leaders must plan extensively for the recruitment, orientation, training, and ongoing support of these individuals to teach in the cluster setup. Program leaders also need to be thoughtful in recruiting faculty to these programs and willing to plan for predictable changes when faculty members take leaves or sabbaticals or make commitments to other courses. Some programs require coordination between faculty members and student affairs professionals or between faculty and peer facilitators. In many models, just three or four teachers coordinate a given cluster; however, at Texas A&M-Corpus Christi as many as ten to twelve faculty members and teaching assistants staff each triad offering. These programs require not only student collaboration but also faculty collaboration, or faculty-staff collaboration.

Learning Communities as Teaching Communities

Obviously, these attempts to create structures that foster connections—among students, with coursework, with faculty or peer facilitators, and with their institutions—have been put in place to foster greater learning on the part of the *students,* and increased *student* success in college. Evaluation data on these programs indicate that they live up to their intentions. What we have yet to give emphasis to or evaluate is how these programs affect the faculty, staff, and students who create and deliver them. We also have yet to assess the impact these programs will have, over time, on the institutions in which they reside.

As many involved with cooperative and collaborative learning have commented, small-group learning can be powerful for students. It brings the otherwise private acts of understanding and reasoning, responding and questioning out into the open, into the sometimes unpredictable glare of public scrutiny (Whipple, 1987; MacGregor, 1990; Millis and Cottell, 1998). Although this can be unfamiliar and challenging, especially at first, these collaborative learning experiences can also be provocative, informative, and valuable—that is, the stuff of long-lasting learning.

The collaborative teaching that occurs in these kinds of programs is not dissimilar. It takes our otherwise private acts of solo teaching into a new arena of shared responsibility, shared students, and often shared curriculum. Through this collaboration often comes immediate feedback on the learning and dynamics that are unfolding week by week. This very public work can be unfamiliar and challenging too, as well as intriguing and valuable.

We hear repeatedly from the faculty members, students, and student affairs professionals involved in these programs how worthwhile it is to teach in them. They describe how team-planning or team-teaching a program opens fascinating windows on their discipline and their teaching. They speak about feeling connected to a larger enterprise. They reflect on the value of working closely with colleagues. They point to the sense of belonging they feel in a large, sometimes faceless institution. These comments remind us that it is not just students who feel alienated by large-class environments. Faculty, staff members, and teaching assistants are affected too. The new collaborative structures require a great deal of energy to create and sustain, yet they create important pockets of community as well as a vision of deeper practice in our institutions.

References

Alexander, B. B., Burda, A. C., and Millar, S. B. "A Community Approach to Learning Calculus: Fostering Success for Underrepresented Ethnic Minorities in an Emerging Scholars Program." *Journal of Women and Minorities in Science and Engineering*, 1997, *3*, 145–159.

Astin, A. W. *What Matters in College? Four Critical Years Revisited.* San Francisco: Jossey-Bass, 1993.

Bonsangue, M. V. "An Efficacy Study of the Calculus Workshop Model." *CBMS Issues in Mathematics Education*, 1994, *4*, 117–137.

Bonsangue, M. V., and Drew, D. E. "Increasing Minority Students' Success in Calculus." In J. Gainen and E. W. Willemsen (eds.), *Increasing Student Success in Quantitative Gateway Courses*. New Directions for Teaching and Learning, no. 61. San Francisco: Jossey-Bass, 1995.

Chickering, A. W., and Gamson, Z. F. "Seven Principles for Good Practice in Undergraduate Education." *American Association for Higher Education Bulletin*, 1987, *39*, 3–7.

Chickering, A. W., and Gamson, Z. F. (eds). *Applying the Seven Principles for Good Practice in Undergraduate Education*. New Directions for Teaching and Learning, no. 47. San Francisco: Jossey-Bass, 1991.

Fullilove, R. E., and Treisman P. U. "Mathematics Achievement Among African American Undergraduates at the University of California, Berkeley: An Evaluation of the Mathematics Workshop Program." *Journal of Negro Education*, 1990, *59*(3), 463–478.

Gabelnick, F., MacGregor, J., Matthews, R., and Smith, B. L. *Learning Communities: Creating Connections Among Students, Faculty, and Disciplines*. New Directions for Teaching and Learning, no. 41. San Francisco: Jossey-Bass, 1990.

George Mason University. *Linked Courses: Observations from Faculty Journals, Fall 1995*. Fairfax, Va.: George Mason University Institutional Assessment Report, 1996.

Johnson, D. W., and Johnson, R. T. *Cooperation and Competition: Theory and Research*. Edina, Minn.: Interaction Books, 1989.

Johnson, W. C. "Freshman Interest Groups (FIGs) Versus Non-FIGs on Scales and Items from Fall 1997 House Environment Survey." Columbia: University of Missouri, 1998 (internal document).

Kosciuk, S. "Impact of the Wisconsin Emerging Scholars First-Semester Calculus Program on Grades and Retention from Fall 1993–1996." Madison: LEAD Center, University of Wisconsin, July 1997.

Light, R. *Harvard Assessment Seminars: Explorations with Students and Faculty About Teaching, Learning, and Student Life*. Cambridge, Mass.: Harvard University, 1992.

Lowell, N. *Freshman Interest Groups, Autumn 1996: Faculty Survey*. Seattle: Office of Educational Assessment, University of Washington, Mar. 1997.

MacGregor, J. "Collaborative Learning: Shared Inquiry as a Process of Reform." In M. Svinicki (ed.), *The Changing Face of College Teaching*. New Directions for Teaching and Learning, no. 42. San Francisco, Jossey-Bass, 1990.

Martin, D., and Arendale, D. (eds.). *Supplemental Instruction: Increasing Achievement and Retention*. New Directions for Teaching and Learning, no. 60. San Francisco: Jossey-Bass, 1994.

Millis, B. J., and Cottell, P. G., Jr. *Cooperative Learning for Higher Education Faculty*. Phoenix: Oryx Press, 1998.

Moreno, S. E., Muller, C., Asera, R., Wyatt, L., and Epperson, J. "Supporting Minority Mathematics Achievement: The Emerging Scholars Program at the University of Texas at Austin." *Journal of Women and Minorities in Science and Engineering*, 1999, 5(1), 53–66.

NIE Study Group on the Conditions of Excellence in Higher Education. *Involvement in Learning: Realizing the Potential of Higher Education*. Washington, D.C.: National Institute of Education, 1984.

Pascarella, E. T., and Terenzini, P. T. *How College Affects Students*. San Francisco: Jossey-Bass, 1991.

Pike, G. R., Schroeder, C. C., and Berry, T. R. "The Effect of Residential Learning Communities on Student Success at a Large Research University." Paper presented at the annual meeting of the Association for the Study of Higher Education, Memphis, Nov. 1, 1996.

Schroeder, C. C., and Hurst, J. C. "Designing Learning Environments That Integrate Curricular and Cocurricular Experiences." *Journal of College Student Development*, 1996, 37(2), 174–181.

Springer, L., Stanne, M., and Donovan, S. "Effects of Small-Group Learning on Undergraduates in Science, Mathematics, Engineering, and Technology: A Meta-Analysis." *Review of Educational Research*, 1999, 69(1), 50–80.

Summerfield, J. *The Freshman Year Initiative at Queens College: A Brief Introduction*. Flushing, N.Y.: Queens College, 1998.

Tinto, V. "Classrooms as Communities: Exploring the Educational Character of Student Persistence." *Journal of Higher Education*, 1997, 68(6), 599–623.

Tinto, V., and Goodsell, A. "Freshman Interest Groups and the First Year Experience: Constructing Student Communities in a Large University." University Park, Pa.: National Center on Postsecondary Teaching, Learning, and Assessment, 1993. (ED 358 778)

Tokuno, K., and Campbell, F. "The Freshman Interest Group Program at the University of Washington: Effects on Retention and Scholarship." *Journal of the Freshman Year Experience*, 1992, 4(1), 7–22.

Treisman, U. "A Study of the Mathematics Performance of Black Students at the University of California, Berkeley." *Dissertation Abstracts International,* 1986, 47, 1641A.

Treisman, U. "Studying Students Studying Calculus: A Look at the Lives of Minority Mathematics Students in College." *College Mathematics Journal,* 1992, 23(5), 362–372.

Whipple, W. "Collaborative Learning: Recognizing It When We See It." *American Association of Higher Education Bulletin,* Oct. 1987, 40(2), 3–7.

5

Developing and using small-group approaches takes time and practice. In this chapter, our faculty informants answer some of the most frequently asked questions about implementing these strategies and overcoming challenges.

Implementing Small-Group Instruction: Insights from Successful Practitioners

James L. Cooper, Jean MacGregor, Karl A. Smith, Pamela Robinson

As we talked with faculty members around the country who are enlivening their classes with small-group work, they described their approaches with enthusiasm and confidence. Yet faculty members who are skeptical about these approaches, and even those tentatively interested in trying them, still raise important concerns about both the philosophy and the actual strategies of undertaking group work. "It really can't be that easy, can it?" they ask, quite rightfully.

A frequent concern that surfaces in many discussions about small-group learning has to do with the assumption that if you are in favor of it, you are de facto opposed to the lecture in any form. This presumption of the new truth is hardly the attitude that will bring about the kind of institutional change that we are hoping for in the coming years. All the teachers we interviewed believe deeply in small-group learning but also spend a significant amount of time lecturing, leading whole-class discussions, and engaging in other kinds of teaching approaches. This is our practice as well. Lecture and small-group work must be framed as both/and endeavors, not either/or ones; yet somehow the message is too often sent that to be in favor of small-group learning is to be completely anti-lecture.

In this chapter we will address a number of concerns about using small-group work that have emerged in the professional literature and that we have encountered as we discussed this approach with colleagues. We will address these concerns based in part on our reading of the literature, but more particularly on the experiences of the practitioners whose approaches are featured in this volume.

Reduced Content Coverage

Aren't you sacrificing content coverage? Class time spent doing group work is certainly time taken from lecturing.

This question comes up most often in discussions about the value of the time spent in groups in class. It speaks to a central issue that has served as a flash point in higher-education circles as articulated by Barr and Tagg in their influential article in *Change* magazine (1995), which called for moving from a teaching to a learning paradigm. We agree with Barr and Tagg that it is more productive to think about the teaching/learning process from the perspective of the gains learners make over the duration of a class rather than from the perspective of what we teachers cover. If cognitive and affective student gains are the measures of success for teachers, then both anecdotal and research evidence appear to lean strongly to using significant amounts of group work, rather than lecturing alone, as we have outlined in Chapter One and will further detail in Chapter Six.

The faculty members we interviewed expressed consistent satisfaction that students in their classes are demonstrating one or more of these indicators of increased learning: much greater conceptual understanding, more complex critical-thinking skills, better class attendance, more independence in lab settings, and greater confidence.

About two-thirds of the faculty members we interviewed said that they covered fewer topics in class when they used group work, but that students learned and retained more of the "big ideas" that they chose to address relative to using lecture formats. Deborah Allen (biology, University of Delaware) said that she suffered from "coveritis" anxiety when she first moved from a lecture format to a group-work approach. "It forced me to take a hard look at the course content, and make good decisions about what the students really needed, versus what I liked to talk about" (Deborah Allen, personal interview with the authors, Feb. 1999). In speaking of reformatting her biology classes from the lecture to small-group work, Patricia Hauslein (biology, St. Cloud University) noted that "if we give them tiny bits of everything, all they will have is rubble. We want to give them the framework, and then they can fill in the floor plan" (Patricia Hauslein, personal interview with the authors, Sept. 1998).

A few years ago Jim Cooper was giving a workshop on small-group work. One faculty member was clearly unhappy with the half-day presentation on various cooperative-learning techniques. Finally, the exasperated participant said, "I teach Biology 101. If I don't cover the content of all seventeen chapters of the textbook, students won't be prepared for Biology

102." When Cooper asked how happy the Biology 102 teachers were with the current graduates of Biology 101, the participant said, "They say that the 102 students don't know anything." This is an extreme example, but we believe that if faculty members will use student performance as the primary criterion of success, adding active and small-group learning to the classroom will follow.

One faculty team, colleagues of Jean MacGregor, addressed this issue head-on when they moved to adopt small-group approaches in their Biology 101 class. They invited the rest of their small biology department out to breakfast and explained their new approach. Then they told their colleagues that the new method would indeed sacrifice some lecture coverage, and they asked them what biological concepts were the most essential, non-negotiable ones for the students to understand well before they entered advanced biology classes. The list of essential understandings, generated on a paper napkin, not only became the driver for the Bio 101 course design but involved everyone in the department in an important beginning discussion about learning outcomes. Even more significantly, it began a process of trust-building with the course reformers.

Reduced Amount of Learning

Do students learn as much using small-group approaches? Is there evidence of this?

We noted in Chapter One the evidence of the power of small-group learning. Work by Ebert-May, Brewer, and Allred (1997), Heller, Keith, and Anderson (1992), Wright (1996), O'Donnell and Dansereau (1992), Mazur (1997), Springer, Stanne, and Donovan (1999), Johnson and Johnson (1989), and others represent formal evidence of the power of small-group work as reported in the college teaching and learning literature. These studies build on hundreds of precollegiate studies demonstrating the power of small-group learning on a host of student outcomes.

Our informants repeatedly told us that their students were performing as well as or better than students in previous teaching settings when small-group activities were not used. All expressed satisfaction that their students are generally demonstrating stronger conceptual understanding, critical thinking skills, and attendance; more independence in a lab setting; and a greater sense of confidence. Diane Ebert-May (botany and plant pathology, Michigan State University) believes that faculty members nationwide must take much more seriously the systematic investigation of whether and what students are actually learning. As she puts it, "The biggest frustration for me is that most faculty members are not using the same empirical approach in their teaching that they are employing in their research" (Ebert-May, personal interview with the authors, July 1998).

Need for Prerequisite Learning

Don't you have to teach students certain information before they work in groups?

About half of those we interviewed agreed that lecturing, reading of material, or other preparatory work should precede group work. Cathy Bristow (entomology, Michigan State University) said, "I agree with this. Students can brainstorm problems, but if they don't have any of the necessary foundation information, just talking about it rapidly loses any utility" (Cathy Bristow, personal interview with the authors, Jan. 1999). Bristow called for a balance between lecturing on foundational concepts and small-group work to apply the concepts. Jim Cooper lectures during the first sixty to ninety minutes of his three-hour classes in graduate educational research methods, then students solve problems (closely linked to the lectures) from a workbook he wrote with Pamela Robinson. He feels that providing a lecture prior to group problem solving ensures that all members of the groups have at least some common experience, which helps them work constructively in teams. Farah Fisher (computer-based education, California State University, Dominguez Hills) has students take a five- or ten-minute quiz at the start of every weekly class to help ensure that they have read the homework assignment prior to doing any group work.

In contrast, approximately half of the faculty members that we talked with felt that this was a ridiculous question. However, many of these teachers use small-group activities to launch students into new material: they present an interesting question or puzzling problem as a strategy to stimulate the students' curiosity and elicit their current conceptual understanding of a topic—essentially, they are laying a foundation for the reading or lecture material to build on. These teachers felt that students could construct their own meaning from relatively new material. Diane Ebert-May said, "That question is loaded with assumptions. It assumes that if you are telling students something, they understand it. This just isn't confirmed by theory. A learner gets to content through creating the mental frameworks for placing the content. It's up to us [teachers] to enable the student to create the frameworks" (Diane Ebert-May, personal interview with the authors, July 1998).

Importance of Solitary Learning

Learning is a solo activity. I had to learn it by myself; therefore students have to learn it by themselves.

Many of those we interviewed disagreed vehemently with this notion. Ray Lischner (computer science, Oregon State University) indicated that professors, who have doctorates and a lifelong commitment to their disciplines, commit an unpardonable sin of teaching when they assume that the students are just like themselves. He says, "Someone with that attitude should be kept as far from the students as possible" (Ray Lischner, personal interview with the authors, Oct. 1998). Diana Archibald (English, University of Massachusetts-Lowell) suspects that professors with that attitude are inclined to underrate students' abilities. "I think you get what you expect from them. If you expect students not to know too much, well, they pick up on this, and they don't become actively engaged" (Diana Archibald, personal interview with the authors, Jan. 1999). Patricia Hauslein cites Parker Palmer's notion that truth is arrived at by collaborative conversations. She says, "I talk about the fact that truth is not owned individually; the truth is agreed upon by communities of people. And I remind students that biology has a strong history of research teams" (Patricia Hauslein, personal interview with the authors, Sept. 1998).

As noted earlier, many of those we interviewed suggested a balance between group and individual work. John Wright (chemistry, University of Wisconsin-Madison) said, "Both extremes are wrong. . . . Cooperative learning is effective but solo activities are also necessary" (John Wright, personal interview with the authors, Oct. 1998). Kay Hudspeth (Maximizing Engineering Potential Program, California State Polytechnic University, Pomona) indicated that some individual learning is appropriate but that students need to "check out what they know with their peers" (Kay Hudspeth, personal interview with the authors, Oct. 1998).

Jean MacGregor, Karl Smith, Jim Cooper, and Pamela Robinson do both individual and group activities. For example, in Cooper's research methods class, students in teams critique a journal article in class before they critique articles individually as homework. He also has students read and critique former students' qualitative research proposals in teams before writing their own proposals. We often find that having teams work on problems and other assignments in class before having students complete individual assignments is a kind of helpful scaffolding technique. The complexity of tasks is reduced before individual assessments of competence are required.

Colleagues' Concerns

What challenges or points of concern have you gotten from colleagues?

Many of the faculty members we interviewed described some degree of skepticism (or even hostility) from colleagues, especially at first. Diane Ebert-May noted that some colleagues have felt her approaches are too "touchy-feely," even though her small-group activities involve high degrees of accountability and occupy only a small fraction of the time spent in her classes. This lack of understanding was also reflected when a dean came to observe a young colleague of Jean MacGregor. This biologist was doing fine work in building small-group learning into his introductory biology class. His dean showed up to conduct a formal classroom observation of him at a moment when the entire class was in groups of three talking animatedly through a set of worksheet problems. Glancing quickly at the scene, the dean said to the teacher, "Oh, I see you are doing group work. I will come back another day when you are teaching." One of the saddest examples of a faculty member misunderstanding small-group approaches occurred when Jim Cooper shared with a colleague that he felt underprepared for that night's class. "Just put them in groups," replied his colleague (quite seriously). Fortunately, these tend to be isolated experiences particularly in recent years, as momentum for small-group approaches has grown. Still, we all should recognize that too many of our colleagues regard small-group approaches as frivolous and a waste of time.

A number of faculty members we interviewed indicated that they perceived only minor resistance from colleagues when it came to the use of small-group work. This may reflect a sampling bias on our part because many of those we interviewed have national reputations for being effective teachers, particularly in large classes. These individuals may enjoy such strong reputations that they are less inclined to encounter active resistance from colleagues. More likely, their approaches to teaching (based on our conversations with them) are so coherent and reasoned that resistance is unlikely to emerge among colleagues. In speaking with these informants, we were impressed with their knowledge of teaching and learning. They spoke of how important it is to have clear ideas about what they want their students to learn, thoughtfully structured assignments and teaching strategies to ensure that these goals are achieved, and meaningful assessment strategies to assess the effectiveness of their teaching.

Student Resistance

What problems or points of resistance have you gotten from students?

According to our informants, student resistance to small-group instruction is generally not due to dislike of small-group work as much as dislike for how these strategies are implemented. The faculty members we interviewed indicated that initial resistance among students generally focused on prior bad experiences with poorly planned and executed group work in high school and college. Features of small-group work perceived as contributing to these negative perceptions included lack of clarity in small-group assignments; unclear or unfair grading of small-group work, often associated with excessive group grading without individual accountability for each team member's contributions; inequitable commitments to teams by individual members; poor planning and organization of the group activities; and inadequate introduction or rationale for group work. As noted in Chapter Two, there is a period of adjustment for students (and for faculty members) that should be expected when educators implement many small-group procedures, according to our informants.

Dan Udovic (biology, University of Oregon) stressed the importance of the clarity of assignments and making these assignments at the correct level of difficulty—neither too challenging nor too trivial. He also pointed to the importance of structuring the tasks so that students do not get bogged down in figuring out how to attack the task, thus wasting time for both students and teachers. Udovic said, "The real challenge here is to create a meaningful problem of suitable complexity and to provide enough time for students to work through it" (Dan Udovic, personal interview with the authors, Nov. 1998). Readers interested in constructing problems and other group assignments may want to consult the workbooks and Web sites identified in Chapter Six to find materials that have been field-tested with students.

When it comes to student resistance, we do not think we can underestimate the shifted expectations students have to experience as they begin to understand, see the value in, and invest energy in small-group learning. Students do not arrive at the door with these understandings. If the other classes they attend carry no expectation of group work, it is as though the ground has shifted under them when they arrive at these kinds of interactive classes. We need to make clear to students that a different set of expectations is at work. We are asking students to make several moves (MacGregor, 1990, pp. 25–26):

- From listener, observer, and note taker to active problem solver, contributor, and discussant
- From low to moderate expectations of their preparedness for class to high ones
- From a private presence in the classroom with few risks to a public one with many risks
- From attendance dictated by personal choice to attendance dictated by community expectation
- From competition with peers to cooperative work with them
- From responsibilities and self-definition associated with learning independently to responsibilities and self-definition associated with learning interdependently
- From the notion that teachers and texts are the sole sources of authority and knowledge to the notion that peers, oneself, and the thinking of one's community are additional and important sources of knowledge

Logistics

How do you handle the logistics of using groups in large classes?

Some colleagues wonder about classroom control issues, fearing that once students move from lecture to small-group work it will be difficult to get them back to attending to the lecture. Most of those we interviewed did not find this to be a problem. Many have a signal to return from group work to the lecture, such as raising a hand or simply asking students to stop talking (because several use microphones, their voices can be heard over the students). We have found that if teachers or TAs circulate among the groups, they can easily determine when the groups have completed their discussions and are ready to return to teacher-centered instruction. This monitoring of groups by walking around is also an effective way of ensuring (by the teacher's or TA's presence) that students are on-task.

Most of those we interviewed were not concerned that students will be off-task during group work. They stressed that the tasks have to be well-structured and challenging and that the time allowed should be limited and clearly defined. Diana Archibald noted that "you have to give students clear tasks and make sure they are held accountable. Students need structure. And they need the challenge of producing a product at the end of the group work" (Diana Archibald, personal interview with the authors, Jan. 1999). John Wright indicates that the tasks he gives groups are "concrete, and students know I am calling on people after the group work. . . . I am not going to let them off the hook so they really stay on-task" (John Wright, personal interview with the authors, Oct. 1998).

Helen Place noted, "Occasionally I have a hard time with a class getting them quiet again: the chatter syndrome. Several groups were chatterers and just wouldn't stay on-task, and other students started to complain. I tell students they have a perfect right to ask other students to shut up so they can hear. One time a woman student stood up in the middle of my lecture and shouted at a group behind her to 'be quiet!' The whole class (of four hundred) broke into applause. Normally, I have the mike and simply ask for their attention. That usually quiets them down, because the answer is about to appear, or I start on a new problem. Mostly they are well-behaved" (Helen Place, personal interview with the authors, Sept. 1998).

Our informants did acknowledge, however, that it is not unusual to have a few groups in each class with some communication difficulties and to encounter occasional groups that are outright dysfunctional. Teachers resolve these problems in a variety of ways. Many spoke of setting appropriate guidelines for effective communication and teamwork at the beginning of the course. Others put the responsibility of group functioning on the groups themselves, preferring not to intervene. Some allow groups to "fire" a member who is dysfunctional (usually after repeated offenses of clearly stated guidelines).

We wondered if there were problems in using small groups with specific student populations, including shy students, ESL students, and students of color. We did not find significant numbers of interviewees who felt that these groups experienced particular problems. In fact, several said that small groups were beneficial to those who might be less inclined to contribute in large-class settings. A significant amount of precollegiate research indicates that small-group work may be particularly effective for minority students and women (Johnson and Johnson, 1989). Less work has been done at the collegiate level, but this work tends to support the efficacy of small-group work for minority students and women (Treisman, 1986; Light, 1992; Gilligan, 1982).

Craig Nelson (biology, Indiana University) told us, "It has been a decade since I had a student who was really unable to participate extensively in structured small-group learning (and have only had about three since I began using these techniques thirty years ago). I attribute this to two factors, mainly. First, I make preparation for group work count heavily on the grades and I assess it regularly. Second, I make each group responsible for eliciting reasonable involvement from each student. For example, all group members lose points unless they ask each member what they have written out in the preparation on each key point—the group's first task is to find out where each person starts. I find that these two principles in combination foster extensive involvement of shy students, ESL students, and members of historically underpowered groups: rural whites, students of color, and so on" (Craig Nelson, personal interview with the authors, July 1999).

Diane Ebert-May reports, "When I taught introductory biology to classes of about 350 at Northern Arizona University, Native American students thrived most noticeably in their cooperative groups. Navajo and Hopi students tended to exhibit quiet behavior and traditionally do not make eye contact with adults with whom they are conversing. Knowing this cultural phenomenon, I tried to form cooperative groups in ways that would benefit more reserved students, especially Native Americans. To accomplish this early in the course, I personally invited in a low-key, inconspicuous way, Native American students who sat off by themselves when they entered the classroom to join a group of three that was forming. I encouraged these students of color to join cooperative groups who sat near the front of the classroom, attended class regularly, and appeared to be open and engaged in their roles as students. Often I facilitated the formation of a group that included one adult learner (over twenty-five years old), a Native American student, and two traditional Caucasian students. Student accomplishments in these specially formed cooperative groups suggested that their diversity served as one of their strengths (that is, the value of diversity, both cultural and biological, is one thread of my course). The Native American students completed the course successfully and often earned points well above the class mean, and were the top students in their groups" (Diane Ebert-May, personal interview with the authors, July 1998).

A Hewlett Foundation–funded project under way at the University of Texas-Austin may provide useful data in the coming years because it is looking at the impact of small-group work in very large classes as a strategy for building tolerance and understanding between different groups early in students' college years. The rationale for this project is that students' first-year experiences on the campus are crucial to connecting them to campus life and enabling them to meet and know other students of different backgrounds. And most students' beginning experiences in large universities are in very large-class settings. So UT-Austin is researching what the impact would be if at least some of those large classes emphasized small-group learning. The Hewlett grant, administered by the Office of Graduate Studies and the Center for Teaching Effectiveness, is providing grants to faculty members teaching classes of one hundred students or more to work with their teaching assistants to incorporate small-group activities or redesign their current strategies substantially. The project also includes a data collection component, which will examine students' sense of connectedness to the campus, their learning preferences, and their responses to small-group learning.

Evaluation

Does using small-group instruction change the ways you evaluate students?

All the faculty members we interviewed indicated that when they moved from primary reliance on the lecture to significant amounts of small-group learning their student-assessment techniques also changed dramatically. They spoke of putting more emphasis on *student skills* and *outcomes* and less on content recall assessed through multiple-choice exams.

In revamping his course in biology for nonscience majors, Dan Udovic (personal interview with the authors, Nov. 1998) spoke of moving from a "tell them and test them" mentality to one requiring more writing, more research projects, and more assessment using rubrics for grading projects and position papers. John Wright indicated that his move to small-group work entailed assessments not based on grading on the curve but on a mastery-learning approach, including provisions to redo work based on teacher feedback. He spoke of moving beyond simply solving chemistry problems to having students *explain* their strategies for solving problems.

A number of informants stressed the importance of using a criterion-referenced grading procedure based on actual performance of individual mastery of course content and understanding. Traditional norm-referenced grading (that is, grading on the curve), they noted, defeats the purpose of cooperative strategies and focuses on having students compete against one another for scarce commodities (As and Bs).

In responding to how his assessment strategies have been effected by switching to small-group work, John Wright said (personal interview with the authors, Oct. 1998), "*Lots* of changes! Evaluation is one of the big frontiers in all of this. You are changing a lot more dimensions of the learning process. . . . When you are changing these things, the assessment needs to reflect those changes. Our students are engaged in mastery learning so they can get nearly perfect scores. All their independent work and small-group work is graded. A lot of these assignments are done with mastery learning so if students get it wrong, they can do it again and get points back. So students have more chances to do better, and given the opportunity, they do. I have students do that kind of mastery learning and then have the exams based on their describing the logic in problems they have already worked. I ask, 'What is the science that underlies the strategy that you used in solving that particular problem?' So there is a real incentive to get the problems correct. They are responsible not just for solving the problem but for explaining their strategy for solving it."

Another assessment issue raised by our informants addressed group versus individual course grades. Although students in the small-group procedures described in this volume are encouraged to help one another (a technique called *positive interdependence* in the cooperative-learning literature), most of the course grading is based on individually completed tests and other assignments. Thus, a relatively small percentage of course grading (perhaps 5 to 15 percent) is based on undifferentiated group grades in which all members of a team receive the same grade, regardless of their relative contributions to the team effort. Some of the group work, especially in the informal strategies outlined in Chapter Two, includes no formal grading of any sort. We find that many small-group strategies are perceived by students as so valuable that no grade is required to motivate them.

Many faculty members spoke of informal classroom assessments as vital to the success of small-group work. Diana Archibald spoke of "ink-shedding," a type of minute paper in which students are asked to write (shed ink) on an issue being examined in the course or on the overall teaching methods used in the course. For example, when her class had gone flat in the middle of one semester, she asked students to ink-shed. She found that many of them were sick and facing exams in other classes—information that most instructors would not have gotten with traditional end-of-semester course evaluations.

John Wright spoke of a board of directors composed of six to fifteen students who meet briefly with him on a weekly basis. He finds the feedback from this group invaluable (although as Tom Angelo notes, do not ask for this type of feedback if you cannot deal with the information you may get).

One of the most powerful elements of small-group instruction is its capacity to provide continuous two-way communication between teachers and students. Faculty members are able to receive information from students while there is time to modify instruction and course content as a result of that feedback. Students are able to modify their approaches to course content at earlier stages of the term as a result of the feedback they receive from other students and their teachers. Compare this with a lecture course that has a midterm and a final, where feedback is often given well after it is too late for either teachers or students to address problems.

Use of Teaching Assistants

How are your TAs involved in the kinds of approaches you are using?

Many faculty members we interviewed indicated that supportive TAs were utterly essential to the success of their approaches. They also stated that they were investing significant time in teaching and coaching their TAs to participate fully in coaching and leading small-group activities.

Predictably, they reported that some TAs were very enthusiastic about these approaches; others, less so. Some universities are moving to restructure courses from three lectures–one discussion section each week to two lectures–two discussion sections, or are reconfiguring labs specifically to increase small-group learning time. A few campuses, such as the University of Delaware and the University of Texas-El Paso, are investing in student peer facilitators to work in large classes as coaches-facilitators of small groups. All these efforts require significant commitments of resources.

The importance of appropriate training for TAs was highlighted by Diane Ebert-May: "Cooperative learning needs to be modeled by all participants in a course, especially faculty members and teaching assistants. Therefore, actively involving TAs in all decisions about reforming a course is critical. We structured the professional development program for the teaching assistants to include practice of effective pedagogy (for example, cooperative learning), introduction to the literature about teaching and learning, and development of the laboratories. We met several days before the beginning of each semester and weekly thereafter. The weekly TA meetings modeled cooperative learning, that is each person had a role in the meeting, such as COW (commander of the week—as named by the TAs) and timekeeper. The COW rotated each week with the associated responsibilities of providing an overview of the forthcoming lab, recommending teaching strategies, and approximating a time line for each lab. All of the TAs reflected on their students' learning from the previous week, talked about what worked and what did not work, and made suggestions for changes. I served as the faculty resource person; the TAs were the decision makers within the context of the reformed course. The most striking observation I made each semester was how the TAs grew from dependence on me to interdependence with each other, how they began to see themselves as reflective teachers, and how they began to focus on students as learners. The majority of TAs indicated that because of their involvement in inquiry-based labs, they themselves became better scientists." (Diane Ebert-May, personal interview with the authors, July 1998).

Helen Place noted, "I encourage all of my TAs, both graduate and undergraduate, to come to lecture and help me during the small-group learning. It is important for the TAs to hear my version of the activity and the level of discussion so they can emulate my approach during tutorials. Also, the TAs learn that teaching can be interactive, even in big classes. It is important to me that more students, during the lectures, can ask questions if there are more 'experts' to ask. I've found that more TAs monitoring groups of students, even those hiding in the back row, tend to keep more students on-task. Often students are more willing to ask TAs rather than let me think they are *dumb*. The challenge is that some TAs lead the students astray. They either don't know the answers or they regurgitate something they just learned in a graduate class. I often have the answers to group problems written out before class and provide them to the TAs. When I don't have answers prepared, I encourage the TAs to work as a group and do the problems before they head out to help the students. I find that undergraduate TAs who took their beginning chem classes from me make better helpers than the new graduate students. I also find that these same undergraduate TAs are more likely to run interactive tutorials" (Helen Place, personal interview with the authors, Sept. 1998).

The Question of Time

Doesn't small-group work take more time? Is it worth the time it takes?

Our faculty informants had a wide range of responses to part one of this concern. Some felt that it did not take more preparation time, particularly if more informal procedures such as think-pair-share or ConcepTests were used. Others noted that their time commitments lessened as they gained experience in using groups. Virtually all faculty members said that the benefits were worth the additional time commitments. Tom Lord (biology, Indiana University-Pennsylvania) said, "Isn't that what professors buy into when they signed their contracts . . . providing the best learning experience possible for the students?" (Tom Lord, personal interview with the authors, Jan. 1999). Helen Place (personal interview with the authors, Sept. 1998) commented, "If we can find a better way to do something, isn't that the way to do it?"

Our informants were mostly in agreement that engaging students in group work in class is not something they have all figured out. Developing good tasks, problems, or questions is an ongoing challenge; so is finding the right balance in classes between group discussion and lecture/presentation. This kind of teaching is a continuing learning experience, which presents new issues and challenges constantly. What our faculty informants value most as they work on these issues is colleagues to turn to for support and for ideas, both about approaches and about dealing with problems. They often mentioned how much they valued the support of their TA team, individuals they knew at other campuses, and less frequently, colleagues in their own department or across campus. Those teachers in national networks (most frequently in science, engineering, and mathematics) seem to have benefitted most from sharing ideas with colleagues.

In the next and final chapter we speculate on whether and how the use of small-group learning will become more widespread in college classrooms. We also offer there a list of resources to assist and support those interested in participating in this movement.

References

Astin, A. W. *What Matters in College? Four Critical Years Revisited.* San Francisco: Jossey-Bass, 1993.

Barr, R. B., and Tagg, J. "From Teaching to Learning: A New Paradigm for Undergraduate Education." *Change,* 1995, 27(6), 13–25.

Ebert-May, D., Brewer, C., and Allred, S. "Innovation in Large Lectures–Teaching for Active Learning." *BioScience,* 1997, *47*(9), 601–607.

Gilligan, C. *In a Different Voice.* Cambridge, Mass.: Harvard University Press, 1982.

Heller, P., Keith, R., and Anderson, S. "Teaching Problem Solving Through Cooperative Grouping. Part 1: Group Versus Individual Problem Solving." *American Journal of Physics,* 1992, *69*(7), 627–636.

Johnson, D. W., and Johnson, R. T. *Cooperation and Competition: Theory and Research.* Edina, Minn.: Interaction Books, 1989.

Light, R. J. *The Harvard Assessment Seminars: Second Report.* Cambridge, Mass.: Harvard University Press, 1992.

MacGregor, J. "Collaborative Learning: Shared Inquiry as a Process of Reform." In M. Svinicki (ed.), *The Changing Face of College Teaching.* New Directions for Teaching and Learning, no. 42. San Francisco: Jossey-Bass, 1990.

Mazur, E. *Peer Instruction: A User's Manual.* Englewood Cliffs, N.J.: Prentice Hall, 1997.

O'Donnell, A. M., and Dansereau, D. F. "Scripted Cooperation in Student Dyads: A Method for Analyzing and Enhancing Academic Learning and Performance." In R. Hertz-Lazarowitz and N. Miller (eds.), *The Theoretical Anatomy of Group Learning.* Cambridge: Cambridge University Press, 1992.

Springer, L., Stanne, M. E., and Donovan, S. "Effects of Small-Group Learning on Undergraduates in Science, Mathematics, Engineering, and Technology: A Meta-Analysis." *Review of Educational Research,* 1999, *69*(1), 50–80.

Treisman, U. "A Study of the Mathematics Performance of Black Students at the University of California, Berkeley." *Dissertation Abstracts International,* 1986, *47,* 1641A.

Wright, J. C. "Authentic Learning Environment in Analytical Chemistry Using Cooperative Methods and Open-Ended Laboratories in Large Lecture Courses." *Journal of Chemical Education,* 1996, *73*(9), 827–832.

6

The expansion of small-group learning approaches in large classes depends on both institutional initiatives and grassroots efforts. Here we provide a list of resources for further information about small-group learning and learning communities.

Making Small-Group Learning and Learning Communities a Widespread Reality

Karl A. Smith, Jean MacGregor

As we rethink what it will take to change the learning environment of large classes, we need to think about the changing functions of classes themselves. Since the development and proliferation of books (and college students are the largest consumers of textbooks) and more recently computer-based media and the World Wide Web, students have access to floods of information in ways the professorate of the past could not have imagined. Suddenly we have an opportunity to rethink the goals of classes, especially the large introductory ones, and to reflect about how students access information and might best make meaning from it.

What special opportunities arise when students are asked to gather in one meeting place at the same time? One of the best reasons for bringing people together is to give them chances to learn from and with one another, to practice communicating and working together to accomplish a common task, and to find out more about one another as people. We need to reconceive classes as the unique social spaces that they can be—where students and teachers interact in personally and intellectually stimulating ways.

In this chapter we discuss some of the pressures to expand this kind of innovative work, the pressures holding it back, and the larger prospects for a growing movement toward small-group learning approaches. We also provide a list of some key resources available in print and on the Web.

Pressures to Change

We all know that voices are pressing in on us to do better in undergraduate education (Marchese, 1998; Boyer Commission, 1998; National Science Foundation, 1996; National Research Council, 1999; Potter, 1999). What continues to emerge from a rising tide of reports and recommendations is the value of

- Active construction of knowledge
- Learning by direct experience and inquiry
- Engaging activities, problems, tasks, and projects
- Focused interaction with faculty
- Active, interactive, and cooperative involvement among students
- Development of team work skills
- Development of abilities to communicate with diverse people
- A sense of belonging and community
- Carefully planned and researched uses of technology

Many of the pressures for change are summarized by Barr and Tagg in their article "From Teaching to Learning: A New Paradigm for Undergraduate Education" (1995) and by Johnson, Johnson, and Smith in *Active Learning: Cooperation in the College Classroom* (1991). A comparison of old and new teaching paradigms appeared in Campbell and Smith's *New Paradigms for College Teaching* (1997) and is shown in Table 6.1.

Although faculty members' theories and practices are not nearly as "either/or" as the table indicates, the trends on the new paradigm side of the table seem to be strengthening. The most profound changes seem to be occurring among individual teachers, like those we interviewed. Many faculty members are changing the way they teach out of a deep concern for students and a sense that "there has to be a better way to do this."

Yet at the same time there are pressures not to change—or not to change very dramatically. There are few structural incentives for reducing enrollments in large classes. There are limited resources for the hiring of teaching assistants or undergraduate facilitators, or for their extensive training and support. On some campuses, limited resources means that many lecture halls remain unsuitable for (and even hostile to) small-group activity. Despite some small efforts to the contrary, reward systems at large research institutions still favor published research over teaching innovation. Just recently, two important articles that appeared in *Change* magazine and *About Campus* candidly discuss how difficult change is and how serious we need to get about taking deeper and more cumulative responsibility for students' learning (Barr, 1998; Schneider and Schoenberg, 1999).

Still, even under these difficult conditions, inspiring reforms of large classes are inching forward. In the science, math, and engineering arena, the National Science Foundation is funding major reform projects. In addition,

Table 6.1. Comparison of Old and New Paradigms for College Teaching

	Old Paradigm	New Paradigm
Knowledge	Transferred from faculty to students	Jointly constructed by students and faculty
Students	Passive vessel to be filled by faculty's knowledge	Active constructor, discoverer, transformer of knowledge
Mode of learning	Memorizing	Relating
Faculty purpose	Classify and sort students	Develop students' competencies and talents
Student goals	Complete requirements, achieve certification within a discipline	Grow, focus on continual lifelong learning within a broader system
Relationships	Impersonal relationship among students and between faculty and students	Personal transaction among students and between faculty and students
Context	Competitive individualistic	Cooperative learning in classrooms and cooperative teams among faculty
Climate	Conformity/cultural uniformity	Diversity and personal esteem/cultural diversity and commonality
Power	Faculty holds and exercises power, authority, and control	Students are empowered; power is shared among students and between students and faculty
Assessment	Norm-referenced (i.e., graded "on the curve"); typically multiple choice items; student rating of instruction at end of course	Criterion-referenced; typically performances and portfolios; continual assessment of instruction
Ways of knowing	Logicoscientific	Narrative
Epistemology	Reductionist; facts and memorization	Constructivist; inquiry and invention
Technology use	Drill and practice; textbook substitute; chalk and talk substitute	Problem solving, communication, collaboration, information access, expression
Teaching assumption	Any expert can teach	Teaching is complex and requires considerable training

Source: Adapted from Campbell and Smith, 1997.

with or without grant funding, many campuses are undertaking learning-community curricular offerings that require significant cross-departmental coordination and impressive faculty–student affairs partnerships.

Making Lasting Change

What is the nature of change in higher education and how does it relate to the change to more active, interactive, and cooperative learning environments? The two types of change we see are, first, the more visible, institutional initiatives—some of which are top-down in nature—and second, the less visible individual and grassroots efforts. We think that more of both kinds is needed.

Institutional Initiatives. In our outreach to the faculty members around the country who became the informants for this book, we came upon several systemic, campuswide projects directed to improving large-class teaching.

University of Texas-Austin Small Group Learning Initiatives. Two projects are under way right now at UT-Austin, both involving large-class learning. The graduate school and the Center for Teaching Effectiveness are involved in a Hewlett Foundation–funded project (described in Chapter Five) with the goal of fostering a greater sense of community and tolerance among students early in their college years, primarily through small-group learning activities in large classes. Discovery Learning, a second grant-supported project—this one funded by the Education Advancement Foundation—focuses on supporting faculty members as they develop a variety of active-learning strategies, quite frequently in large introductory classes. Minigrants support faculty and teaching assistants as they develop new approaches, and monthly luncheons provide a venue for gathering new ideas as well as for forming a community of shared practice.

University of Maryland Large Classes Project. A project specifically directed toward improvement of large-class teaching has been under way at the University of Maryland for several years. It began as a continuous quality improvement (CQI) effort charged by the vice president for academic affairs and provost to research and then address the challenges associated with large-class teaching. In a unique move, the vice president created a "cross-functional" team to tackle this problem. The team worked through a careful stepwise data-gathering exercise involving department leaders, faculty members, representatives of the physical plant, and students to understand more fully the problems and root causes with widespread dissatisfaction associated with large classes (see Chapter One for a discussion of this). Their recommendations involved everything from providing ideas and resources to teachers of large classes, to furthering study of the reward structure in large classes, to creating a facilities team to take action on the improvement of physical classroom settings. Ideas distilled from the Center for Teaching Effectiveness's workshops and *The Large Classes*

Newsletter are now available in Elisa Carbone's *Teaching Large Classes: Tools and Strategies* (1998) and a journal article she coauthored (Carbone and Greenberg, 1998).

Michigan State University Active Learning Initiative. Michigan State University has been involved in extensive faculty development work in cooperative learning for the past ten years. The seeds were planted during cooperative learning workshops that were held as part of their Lilly Endowment Teaching Fellows program. Hundreds of faculty members in tens of departments are engaging their students in active, interactive, and cooperative learning during class time. Recently, several faculty members have asked for even more intensive work, and in response advanced cooperative leaning and cooperative learning leadership workshops have been added. MSU leaders have persistently encouraged and supported implementation of the university's "six guiding principles," developed under the stewardship of President Peter McPherson in 1994. In 1999, they developed a series of implementation points, including "the support of additional experimentation with real-world learning strategies such as problem-based learning, cooperative learning, case-based learning, and service learning."

University of Delaware Problem-Based Learning Initiative. The University of Delaware has implemented problem-based learning (PBL) in many introductory courses (described in detail in Chapter Three) and provides weeklong faculty development workshops, teaching assistant training, consultation, and lots of additional follow-up and support. The initiative began in the sciences, physics, and biology, and is spreading across the university. The initiative received extensive external grant support, which helped get it started, but has involved a wide number of faculty members and their teaching assistants.

University of Texas-El Paso: The Model Institutions for Excellence Project. In the border metropolis of El Paso, Texas, and Juarez, Mexico, UTEP is investing a multimillion dollar National Science Foundation grant in major reform of undergraduate science classes. The explicit intention is to enable more Latino students to be successful in entering majors and graduate programs in the sciences and engineering. This very large institution-wide initiative is creating learning-community curricula (described in Chapter Four), a commitment to peer-facilitated small-group learning, a student study center, and opportunities for faculty development and special student internships.

Large-scale changes are hard to sustain at very large institutions such as these. They usually do not occur without a group of colleagues who sustain a vision and then provide continuing support and encouragement for one another. These five institutional stories have common features (put forward in Johnson, Johnson, and Smith, 1998) found to be vitally important in strengthening personal and organizational change:

- These projects identify a clear focus or clear goals. Meaningful change requires teams pulling together to achieve a common goal.

- These projects promote an attitude of experimentation. Change requires an atmosphere in which there is a willingness to try things and learn from what is attempted.
- Finally, these projects create collegial support networks of faculty, students, staff, and administrators.

Grassroots Efforts. Although the institutional efforts are very promising, the more prevalent pattern for change is at the grass roots. A growing community of faculty members scattered in institutions throughout the country are implementing changes on their own or with their teaching assistants in a single course or department. Often this work remains unknown and unheralded on the campuses where it is occurring. We can think of these efforts spreading among users as described in Everett Rogers's now-classic theories about diffusion of innovations, or we might think of these efforts as something a bit more transformative, as Parker Palmer might.

Rogers's diffusion of innovation model is based on an S-curve adoption of innovation as a function of time (Rogers, 1995). It starts with the innovators, progresses to the early adopters (about 14 percent), next to the early majority (about 34 percent), then to the late majority (about 34 percent), and finally to the laggards (about 16 percent). Through a truly modest level of publication, but more frequently through conferences and word of mouth, these approaches have quietly spread around the country among both innovators and early adopters. Overall, the implementation of small-group learning in higher education appears to be well established among the early adopters and perhaps even used by some in the early majority. In very large classes, it is probably more likely the case that only the innovators and some early adopters are using small-group approaches.

Some of these innovative teachers see small-group strategies simply as techniques they practice occasionally, along with an array of other tools. Others see the move into small-group and problem-centered teaching and learning as more transformative. These teachers believe that cooperative and collaborative learning forces us to conceive of student learning in a way that has implications for the very structure of our classes, the training of teaching assistants, and the design of curricula. They see their work as part of a social movement—perhaps even a transformation of education.

The social movement level of change implies that the innovation does not simply spread quietly and get picked up here and there. Rather, it becomes the center of teachers' philosophies of student learning and their practice of teaching. As educational leader Patricia Cross has observed, the biggest and most long-lasting reforms in undergraduate education will come when individual faculty or small groups of instructors adopt a view of themselves as reformers in their immediate sphere of influence: the classes they teach every day (Patricia Cross, personal interview with the authors, July 1999).

Parker Palmer (1997a, 1997b, 1998) pushes us to think even more ambitiously. He recently posed the following question about educational reform: "Is it possible to embody our best insights about teaching and learning in a social movement that might revitalize learning?" (1998, p. 166). From his study of several social justice movements, he observes that movements usually develop in four sequential steps:

- *Stage 1:* Isolated individuals make an inward decision to live "divided no more," finding a center for their lives outside of institutions.
- *Stage 2:* These individuals begin to discover one another and form communities of congruence that offer mutual support and opportunities to develop a shared vision.
- *Stage 3:* These communities of congruence start going public, learning to convert their private concerns into the public issues they are and receiving vital critiques in the process.
- *Stage 4:* A system of alternative rewards emerges to sustain the movement's vision and to put pressure for change on the standard institutional reward system.

A large majority of the individuals we interviewed for this volume spoke as if they truly have made personal decisions to live "divided no more" and to throw themselves into teaching in a new way—even though they teach in some of the most demanding settings in undergraduate education. Admittedly, many we interviewed are pursuing these teaching approaches on their own and report feeling lonely in their departments without the support of or even interest from colleagues. However, numbers of others have indeed found "communities of congruence" to which to turn for ideas, support, and understanding about what works and what needs to be changed. Approaches are being shared through Web sites alone in inspiring and remarkable ways. And without question, many of these teachers are already having a profound influence on their teaching assistants, and this in turn may produce a different new generation of teachers.

So with small-group learning and curricular learning communities, we sense that a small social movement is beginning to emerge. It is somewhere around Palmer's Stage 2 in our estimation, and glimpses of Stage 3 are already on the horizon. As people gravitate to what it takes to foster active learning on the part of students, they begin to go public not just with the innovation they've adopted but with its implications for existing curricular structures and for changing the existing reality. They are becoming more vocal about the need for better classroom architecture that is more conducive to small groups and for "smart" classroom technology. They are restructuring entire courses to reduce lecture and increase discussion and laboratory work, and in so doing are rethinking the training of teaching assistants. They are becoming more vocal about reward systems and structures that honor the work of teaching effectively in these settings, and research and scholarship on student learning as well.

As we reflect on our year of collaborative research on small-group learning in large classes, we are filled with optimism. This inspiring group of faculty innovators are on the leading edge of a new way of conceiving large-class learning. Although the institutional initiatives we discovered are important, it is the growing interest and activity of teachers at the grass roots that lead us to believe that lasting change may really come about. The power of these individuals' energy, vision, and commitment to student learning reminds us of Margaret Mead's often quoted insight: "Never doubt that a small group of thoughtful, committed citizens can change the world. Indeed, it is the only thing that ever has" (Frank, 1999, p. 510).

Additional Resources for Small-Group Learning and Learning Communities

This section includes many of the most common sources on small-group learning in print and on the World Wide Web. A Web site is being developed to provide access to the materials cited; visit Karl Smith's site [www.ce.umn.edu/~smith] to access these resources. Also, we want to hear your feedback! Please e-mail one of the authors with your success stories, comments, or questions: jeanmacg@thurston.com, jcooper@dhvx20.csudh .edu, ksmith@tc.umn.edu, or probinson@dhvx20.csudh.edu.

Theory and Rationales for Small-Group Learning

Bonwell, C. C., and Eison, J. A. "Active Learning: Creating Excitement in the Classroom." ASHE-ERIC Higher Education Report No. 1. Washington, D.C.: George Washington University, 1991.

Belenky, M. F., Clinchy, B. M., Goldberger, N. R., and Tarule, J. M. *Women's Ways of Knowing: The Development of Self, Voice, and Mind.* New York: Basic Books, 1986.

Brooks, J., and Brooks, M. G. *In Search of Understanding: The Case for Constructivist Teaching.* Alexandria, Va.: Association for Supervision and Curriculum Development, 1993.

Bruffee, K. *Collaborative Learning: Higher Education, Interdependence and the Authority of Knowledge.* Baltimore: Johns Hopkins University Press, 1993.

Campbell, W. E., and Smith, K. A. (eds). *New Paradigms for College Teaching.* Edina, Minn.: Interaction Books, 1997.

Derek Bok Center for Teaching and Learning. *Thinking Together Collaborative Learning in the Sciences.* Cambridge, Mass.: Derek Bok Center for Teaching and Learning, Harvard University, 1991. Videocassette.

Gardiner, L. F. "Redesigning Higher Education: Producing Dramatic Gains in Student Learning." ASHE-ERIC Higher Education Report No. 7. Washington, D.C.: The George Washington University, 1994.

Johnson, D. W., and Johnson, R. T. *Cooperation and Competition: Theory and Research.* Edina, Minn.: Interaction Books, 1989.

Johnson, D. W., Johnson, R. T., and Smith, K. A. "Cooperative Learning: Increasing College Faculty Instructional Productivity." ASHE-ERIC Higher Education Report No. 4. Washington, D.C.: The George Washington University, 1991.

Johnson, D. W., Johnson, R. T., and Smith, K. A. "Cooperative Learning Returns to College: What Evidence Is There That It Works?" *Change,* 1998, *30*(4), 26–35.

Katzenbach, J. R., and Smith, D. K. *The Wisdom of Teams: Creating the High Performance Organization.* Cambridge, Mass.: Harvard Business School, 1993.

Kohn, A. *No Contest: The Case Against Competition.* Boston: Houghton-Mifflin, 1986.

Kohn, A. *What to Look for in a Classroom.* San Francisco: Jossey-Bass, 1998.

MacGregor, J. "Collaborative Learning: Shared Inquiry as a Process of Reform." In M. Svinicki (ed.), *The Changing Face of College Teaching*. New Directions for Teaching and Learning, no. 42. San Francisco, Jossey-Bass, 1990.

Matthews, R. S., Cooper, J. L., Davidson, N., and Hawkes, P. "Building Bridges Between Cooperative and Collaborative Learning." *Change*, 1995, 27(4), 35–39.

Springer, L., Stanne, M. E., and Donovan, S. "Effects of Small-Group Learning on Undergraduates in Science, Mathematics, Engineering, and Technology: A Meta-Analysis." *Review of Educational Research*, 1999, 69(1), 50–80.

Stage, F. K., Muller, P. A., Kinzie, J., and Simmons, A. "Creating Learning-Centered Classrooms: What Does Learning Theory Have to Say?" ASHE-ERIC Higher Education Report No. 4. Washington, D.C.: George Washington University, 1998.

Tinto, V. "Classrooms as Communities Exploring the Educational Character of Student Persistence." *Journal of Higher Education*, 1997, 68(6), 599–623.

General Resources on Cooperative and Small-Group Learning

Abrami, P. C., Chambers, B., d'Apollonia, S., De Simone, C., Wagner, D., Poulsen, C., Glashan, A., and Farrell, M. *Using Cooperative Learning*. Montreal, Quebec: Centre for the Study of Classroom Processes, Concordia University, 1990.

Carbone, E., and Greenberg, J. "Teaching Large Classes: Unpacking the Problem and Responding Creatively." In M. Kaplan (ed.), *To Improve the Academy*. Vol. 17. Stillwater, Okla.: New Forums Press and the Professional and Organizational Development Network in Higher Education, 1998.

Cooper, J. L. *Cooperative Learning and College Teaching*. Stillwater, Okla.: New Forums Press, 1999.

Goodsell, A., Maher, M., and Tinto, V. *Collaborative Learning: A Sourcebook for Higher Education*. University Park, Pa.: National Center for Postsecondary Teaching, Learning, and Assessment, 1992.

Johnson, D. W., Johnson, R. T., and Smith, K. A. *Active Learning: Cooperation in the College Classroom* (2nd ed.). Edina, Minn: Interaction Books, 1998a.

Johnson, D. W., Johnson, R. T., and Smith, K. A. "Maximizing Instruction Through Cooperative Learning." *ASEE Prism*, 1998b, 7(6), 24–29.

Kadel, S., and Keehner, J. A. *Collaborative Learning: A Sourcebook for Higher Education*. Vol. II. University Park, Pa.: National Center for Postsecondary Teaching, Learning, and Assessment, 1994.

Millis, B. J., and Cottell, P. G. Jr. *Cooperative Learning for Higher Education Faculty*. Phoenix: Oryx Press, 1998.

Nevin, A., Smith, K. A., and Udvari-Solner, A. "Cooperative Group Learning and Higher Education." In J. Thousand, R. Villa, and A. Nevin (eds), *Creativity and Collaborative Learning: A Practical Guide to Empowering Students and Teachers*. Baltimore: Paul H. Brookes, 1994.

Smith, K. A. "Cooperative Base Groups: Building Community and Involvement." *Faculty Development*, 1997, 11(1), 6.

Smith, K. A., Johnson, D. W., and Johnson, R. T. "Structuring Learning Goals to Meet the Goals of Engineering Education." *Engineering Education*, 1981, 70, 221–226.

Sutherland, T. E., and Bonwell, C. C. (eds.). *Using Active Learning in College Classes: A Range of Options for Faculty*. New Directions for Teaching and Learning, no. 67. San Francisco: Jossey-Bass, 1996.

Tiberius, R. G. *Small Group Teaching: A Trouble-shooting Guide*. Toronto: OISE Press, 1990.

General Resources on Large Classes

Carbone, E. *Teaching Large Classes: Tools and Strategies*. Thousand Oaks, Calif.: Sage, 1998.

Gedalof, A. J. *Teaching Large Classes.* Halifax, Nova Scotia: Dalhousie University, 1998.

Mazur, E. *Peer Instruction: A User's Manual.* Englewood Cliffs, N.J.: Prentice-Hall, 1997.

Weimer, M. G. (ed.). *Teaching Large Classes Well.* New Directions for Teaching and Learning, no. 32. San Francisco: Jossey-Bass, 1987.

Cooperative Learning Web Sites

Calculus, Concepts, Computers, and Cooperative Learning at Purdue University [http:// www.math.purdue.edu/~ccc/]

Collaborative Learning: Small Group Home Page—National Institute for Science Education, University of Wisconsin-Madison [http://www.wcer.wisc.edu/nise/cl1/CL /clhome.asp]

The Cooperative Learning Center at the University of Minnesota [http://www.clcrc.com/ or http://www.cooperation.org/]

Cooperative Learning: Response to Diversity [http://www.cde.ca.gov/iasa/cooplrng.html]

Kagan Cooperative Learning Web site [http://www.kagancooplearn.com/]

Richard Felder's Cooperative Learning Web site at North Carolina State University [http://www2.ncsu.edu/unity/lockers/users/f/felder/public/RMF.html]

Listservs on Collaborative Learning and Learning Communities

Temple University hosts two listservs, one on collaborative learning and one on learning communities. To subscribe to the collaborative learning listserv, send a message to collabor@listserv.temple.edu. Leave the subject line blank and in the body of the message, type "subscribe collabor" and then your name. To subscribe to the learning communities list, send a message to learncom@listserv.temple.edu. Leave the subject line blank and in the body of the message, type "subscribe learncom" and your name.

Resources on Specific Approaches

Case Method

Barnes, L. B., Christensen, C. R., and Hansen, A. J. *Teaching and the Case Method: Text, Cases, and Readings* (3rd ed.). Cambridge, Mass.: Harvard Business School, 1994.

Christensen, C. R. *Teaching by the Case Method.* Cambridge, Mass: Harvard Business School, 1981.

Christensen, C. R., Garvin, D. A., and Sweet, A. *Education for Judgment: The Artistry of Discussion Leadership.* Cambridge, Mass.: Harvard Business School, 1991.

Classroom Assessment

Angelo, T. A. *Classroom Assessment and Research: An Update on Uses, Approaches, and Research Findings.* New Directions for Teaching and Learning, no. 75. San Francisco: Jossey-Bass, 1998.

Angelo, T. A., and Cross, K. P. *Classroom Assessment Techniques: A Handbook for College Teachers* (2nd ed.). San Francisco: Jossey-Bass, 1993.

Controversy

Johnson, D. W., and Johnson, R. T. *Creative Controversy: Intellectual Challenge in the Classroom.* Edina, Minn: Interaction Books, 1995.

Johnson, D. W., Johnson, R. T., and Smith, K. A. "Academic Controversy: Enriching College Instruction Through Intellectual Conflict." ASHE-ERIC Higher Education Report No. 3. Washington, D.C.: The George Washington University, 1996.

Jigsaw

Aronson, E., Blaney, N., Stephan, C., Sikes, J., and Snapp, M. *The Jigsaw Classroom.* Thousand Oaks, Calif.: Sage, 1978.

Learning Communities

Gabelnick, F., MacGregor, J., Matthews, R., and Smith, B. L. *Learning Communities: Creating Connections Among Students, Faculty, and Disciplines.* New Directions for Teaching and Learning, no. 41. San Francisco: Jossey-Bass, 1990. (*Note:* An expanded version of this book will be published by Jossey-Bass early in 2001.)

Levine, J. H. (ed.). *Learning Communities: New Structures, New Partnerships for Learning.* Columbia: University of South Carolina, National Resource Center for the First-Year Experience and Students in Transition, 1999.

Shapiro, N., and J. H. Levine. *Creating Learning Communities: A Practical Guide to Winning Support, Organizing for Change, and Implementing Programs.* San Francisco: Jossey-Bass, 1999.

Washington Center for Undergraduate Education, Evergreen State College Web site [http://www.evergreen.edu/washcenter/]

Problem-Based Learning

Boud, D., and Feletti, G. E. *The Challenge of Problem-Based Learning* (2nd ed.). London: Kogan Page, 1997.

Delisle, R. *How to Use Problem-Based Learning in the Classroom.* Alexandria, Va.: Association for Supervision and Curriculum Development, 1997.

Rhem, J. "Problem-Based Learning: An Introduction." *National Teaching and Learning Forum,* 1998, 8(1), 1–3.

Wilkerson, L., and Gijselaers, W. H. (eds.). *Bringing Problem-Based Learning to Higher Education: Theory and Practice.* New Directions for Teaching and Learning, no. 68. San Francisco: Jossey-Bass, 1996.

Woods, D. R. *Problem-Based Learning: How to Gain the Most from PBL.* Waterdown, Ontario: Donald R. Woods, 1994.

Problem-Based Learning Web Sites

Illinois Math and Science Academy
    [http://www.imsa.edu/team/cpbl/cpbl.html]
McMaster University Chemical Engineering
    [http://chemeng.mcmaster.ca/pbl/pbl.htm]
Samford University
    [http://LR.Samford.edu/PBL/]
Southern Illinois School of Medicine
    [http://edaff.siumed.edu/PBLI/pblisiu.htm]
University of Delaware
    [http://www.udel.edu/pbl/]

Supplemental Instruction

Martin, D., and Arendale, D. R. (eds.). *Supplemental Instruction Increasing Achievement and Retention.* New Directions for Teaching and Learning, no. 60. San Francisco, Jossey-Bass, 1994.

University of Missouri-Kansas City Web site
    [www.umkc.edu/cad/]

References

Barr, R. B. "Obstacles to Implementing the Learning Paradigm—What It Takes to Overcome Them." *About Campus,* 1998, 3(4), 18–25.

Barr, R. B., and Tagg, J. "From Teaching to Learning: A New Paradigm for Undergraduate Education." *Change,* 1995, 27(6), 13–25.

Boyer Commission. "Reinventing Undergraduate Education: A Blueprint for America's Research Universities." [http://notes.cc.sunysb.edu/Pres/boyer.nsf]. 1998.

Campbell, W. E., and Smith, K. A. (eds.). *New Paradigms for College Teaching.* Edina, Minn.: Interaction Books, 1997.

Carbone, E. *Teaching Large Classes: Tools and Strategies.* Thousand Oaks, Calif.: Sage, 1998.

Carbone, E., and Greenberg, J. "Teaching Large Classes: Unpacking the Problem and Responding Creatively." In M. Kaplan (ed.), *To Improve the Academy.* Vol. 17. Stillwater, Okla.: New Forums Press and the Professional and Organizational Development Network in Higher Education, 1998.

Frank, L. R. (ed.). *Random House Webster's Quotationary.* New York: Random House, 1999.

Johnson, D., Johnson, R. T., and Smith, K. A. *Active Learning: Cooperation in the College Classroom* (1st ed.). Edina, Minn.: Interaction Books, 1991.

Johnson, D., Johnson, R. T., and Smith, K. A. *Active Learning: Cooperation in the College Classroom* (2nd ed.). Edina, Minn.: Interaction Books, 1998.

Marchese, T. "Not-So-Distant Competitors: How New Providers Are Remaking the Postsecondary Marketplace." *American Association for Higher Education Bulletin,* 1998, 50(9), 3–7.

National Research Council. *Transforming Undergraduate Education in Science, Mathematics, Engineering and Technology.* Washington, D.C.: National Academy Press, 1999.

National Science Foundation. "Shaping the Future: New Expectations for Undergraduate Education in Science, Mathematics, Engineering, and Technology." A report by the advisory committee on its review of undergraduate education (NSF 96–139). Arlington, Va.: National Science Foundation, 1996.

Palmer, P. J. "Teaching and Learning in Community." *About Campus,* 1997a, 2(5), 4–13.

Palmer, P. J. "The Heart of a Teacher: Identity and Integrity in Teaching." *Change,* 1997b, 29(6), 14–22.

Palmer, P. J. *The Courage to Teach: Exploring the Inner Landscape of a Teacher's Life.* San Francisco: Jossey-Bass, 1998.

Potter, D. L. "Where Powerful Partnerships Begin." *About Campus,* 1999, 4(2), 11–16.

Rogers, E. M. *Diffusion of Innovations* (4th ed.). New York: Free Press, 1995.

Schneider, C. G., and Shoenberg, R. "Habits Hard to Break: How Persistent Features of Campus Life Frustrate Curricular Reform." *Change,* 1999, 31(2), 30–35.

INDEX

Back Issue/Subscription Order Form

Copy or detach and send to:
Jossey-Bass Inc., Publishers, 350 Sansome Street, San Francisco CA 94104-1342

Call or fax toll free!
Phone 888-378-2537 6AM-5PM PST; Fax 800-605-2665

Back issues: Please send me the following issues at $23 each
(Important: please include series initials and issue number, such as TL90)

1. TL _____

_____

_____

$ _____   Total for single issues

$ _____   Shipping charges (for single issues *only;* subscriptions are exempt from shipping charges): Up to $30, add $5^{50} • $30^{01}–$50, add $6^{50} $50^{01}–$75, add $7^{50} • $75^{01}–$100, add $9 • $100^{01}–$150, add $10 Over $150, call for shipping charge

Subscriptions   Please ❑ start   ❑ renew my subscription to *New Directions for Teaching and Learning* for the year _____ at the following rate:

❑ Individual $58   ❑ Institutional $104
NOTE: Subscriptions are quarterly, and are for the calendar year only. Subscriptions begin with the spring issue of the year indicated above. For shipping outside the U.S., please add $25.

$ _____   Total single issues and subscriptions (CA, IN, NJ, NY and DC residents, add sales tax for single issues. NY and DC residents must include shipping charges when calculating sales tax. NY and Canadian residents only, add sales tax for subscriptions)

❑ Payment enclosed (U.S. check or money order only)
❑ VISA, MC, AmEx, Discover Card #_____ Exp. date_____

Signature _____ Day phone _____
❑ Bill me (U.S. institutional orders only. Purchase order required)
Purchase order #_____

Name _____
Address _____

_____

_____

Phone_____ E-mail _____

For more information about Jossey-Bass Publishers, visit our Web site at:
www.josseybass.com   **PRIORITY CODE = ND1**

Strategies for energizing
large classes : from small
groups to learning
communities